4 STEP DRAWING EXAMPLE

When drawing with a pencil, use light lines so that you can easily correct mistakes. Carefully follow the arrows to complete your drawing. Use the empty space to experiment to get a better drawing.

AUDIO-PLAYER **PRACTICE**

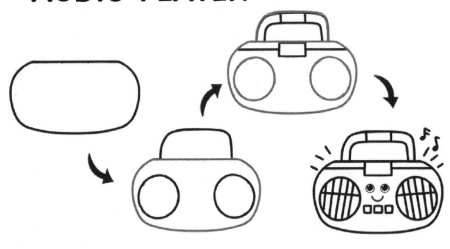

This book belongs

_____

_____

ISBN: 9798300984663
Copyright © 2024 by Lyra Venn
All rights reserved.
No part of this book can be reproduced in any form of electronic or mechanical means without written permission from the Author.

What's in there

- Cute Stuff
- Animals and Birds
- Food & Drink
- Landscape
- Monster
- Robot Toys and Accessories

Chapter 1: Sweet Things

SOFA — PRACTICE

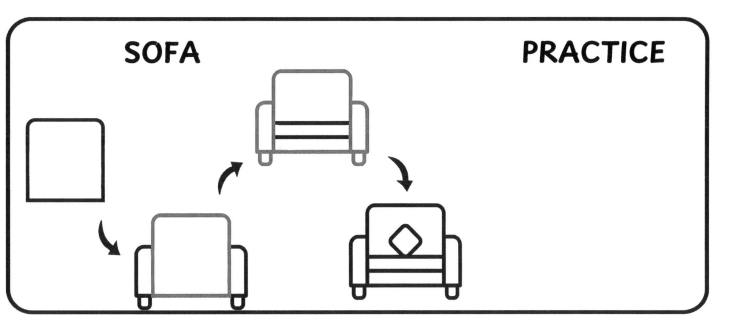

TOY BUCKET — PRACTICE

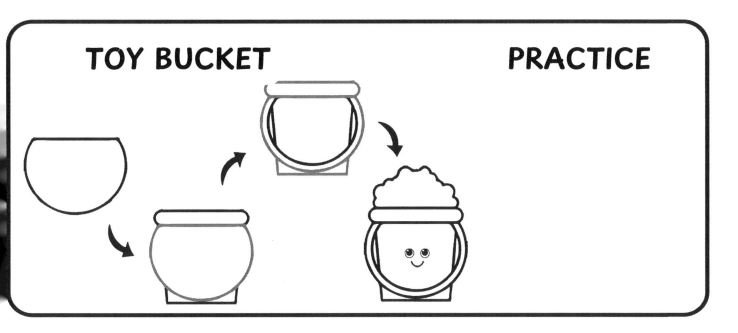

GLUE — PRACTICE

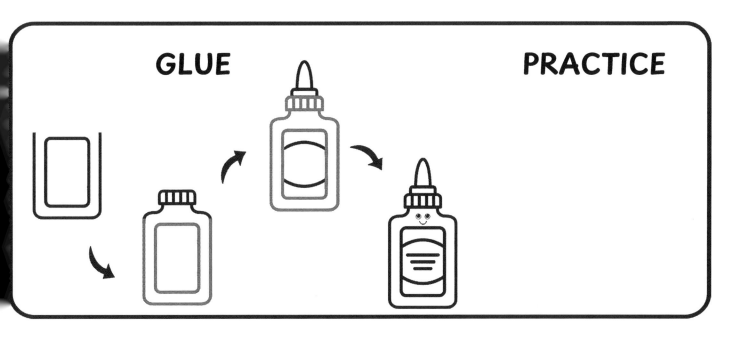

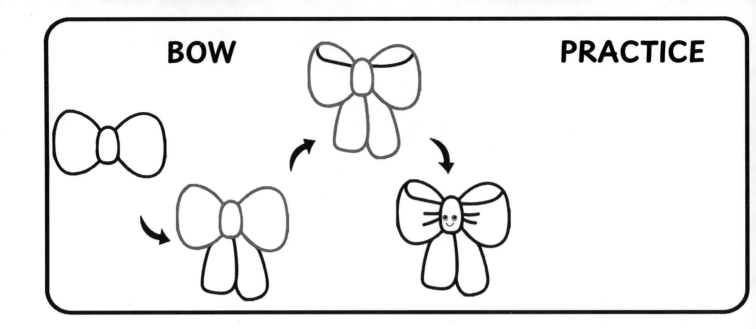

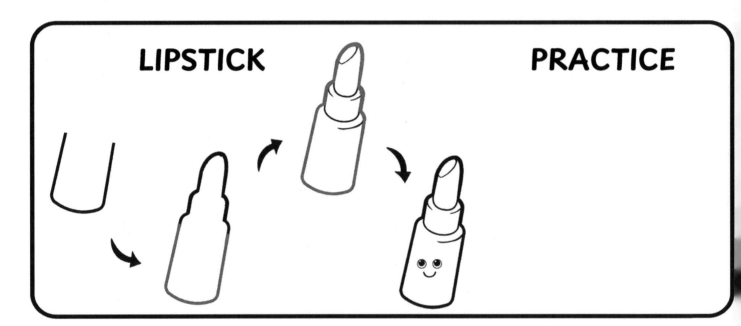

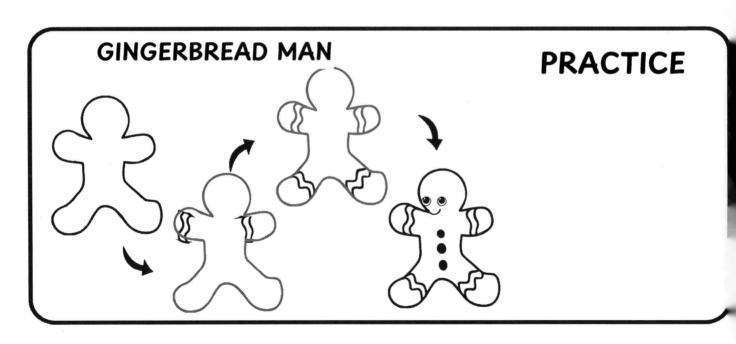

TOYS PRACTICE

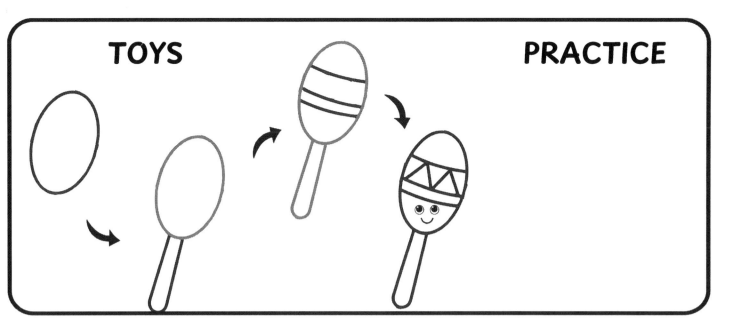

AUDIO PLAYER PRACTICE

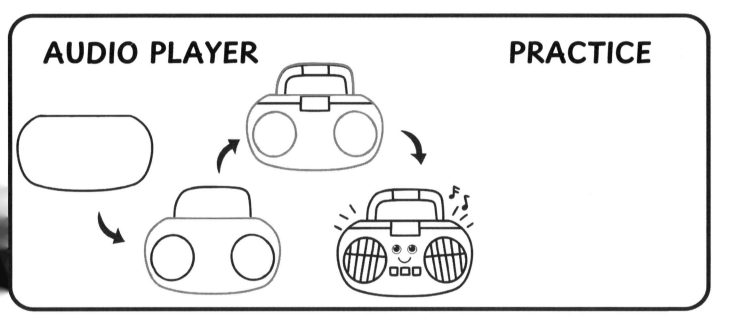

HAIRPIN PRACTICE

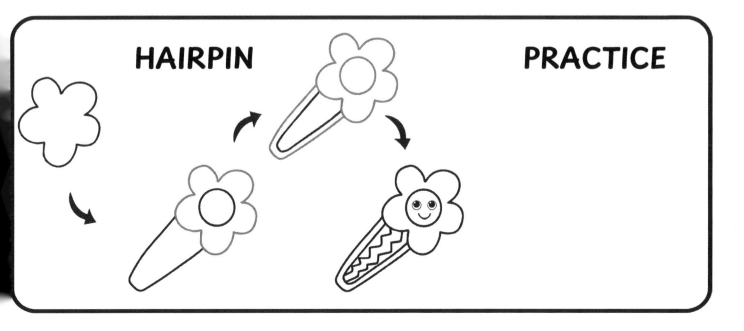

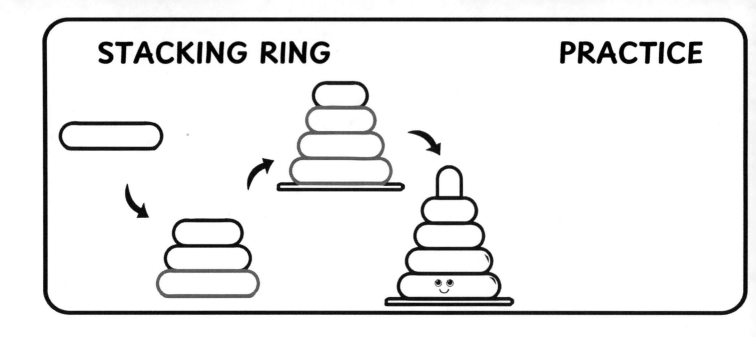
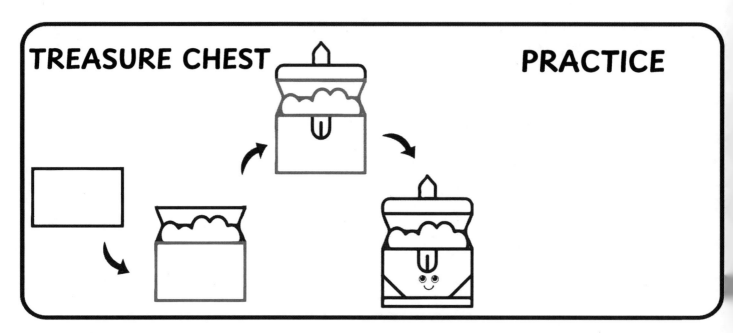
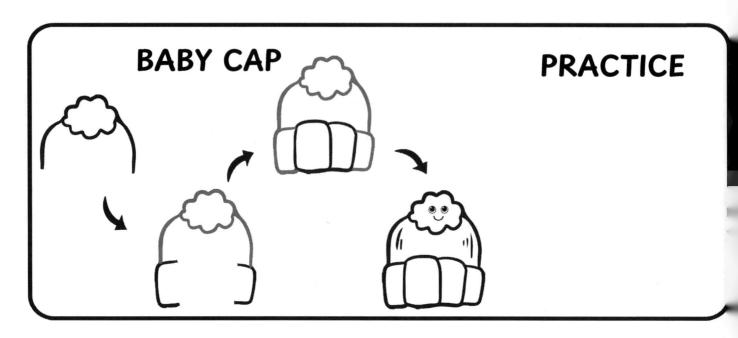

TELEVISION — PRACTICE

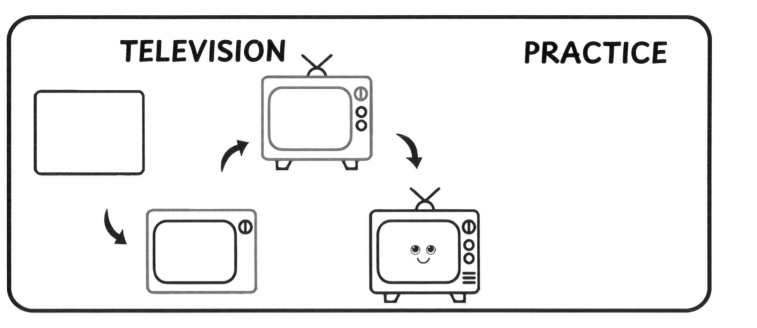

LAMP — PRACTICE

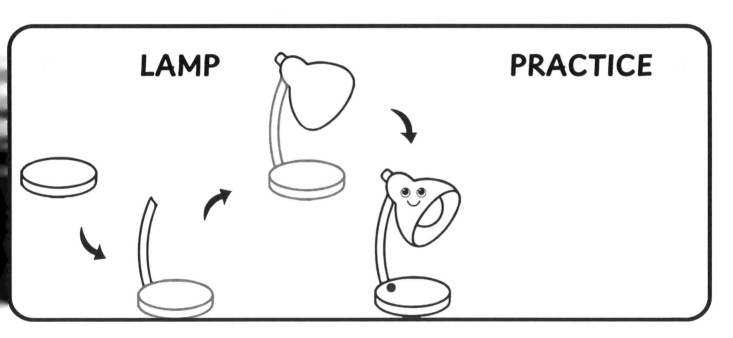

HAMMER — PRACTICE

ROLLER SKATES — PRACTICE

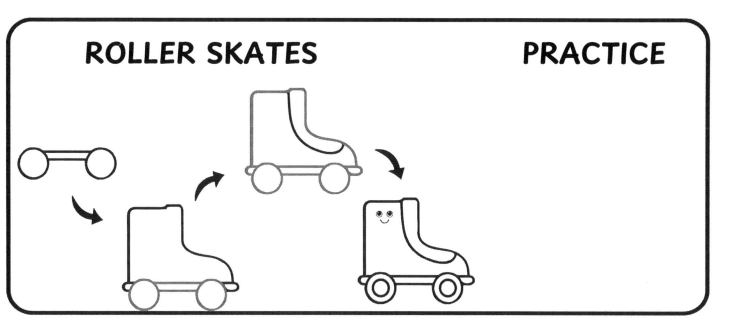

FUNDS — PRACTICE

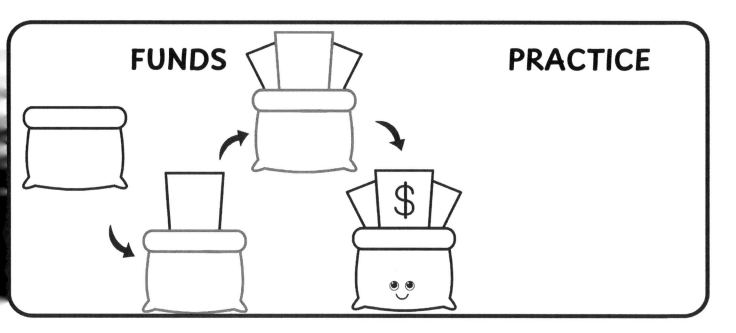

SPY GLASS — PRACTICE

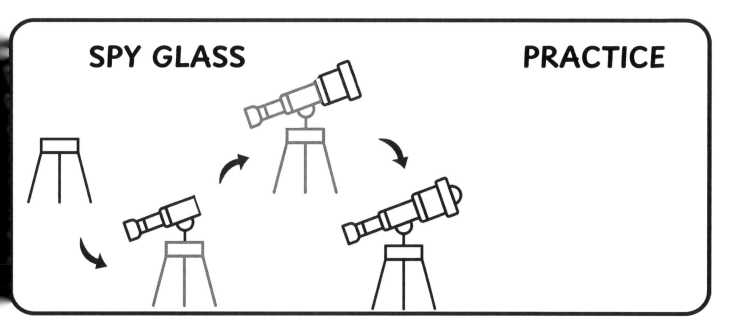

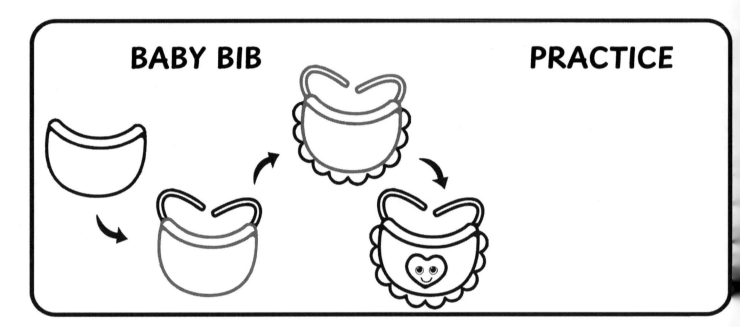

CIRCUS CARNIVAL — PRACTICE

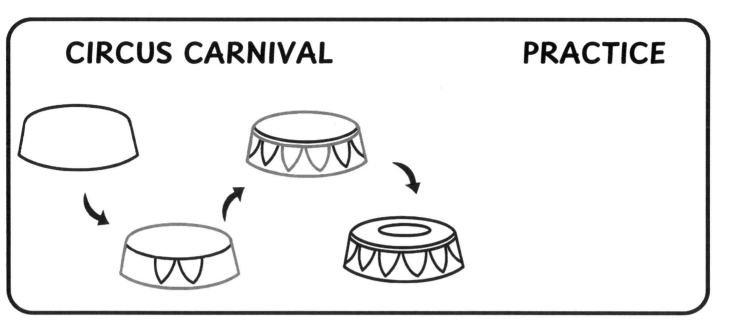

BABY STROLLER — PRACTICE

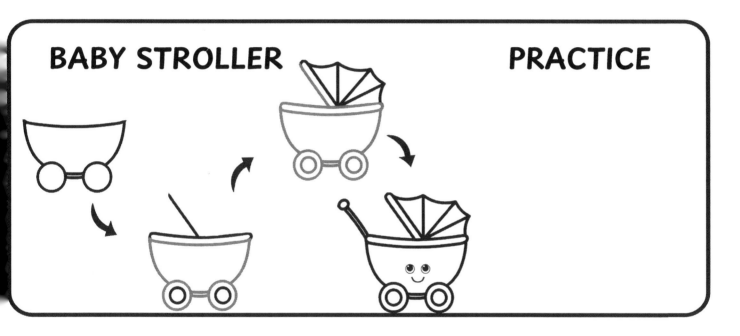

BATH TUB — PRACTICE

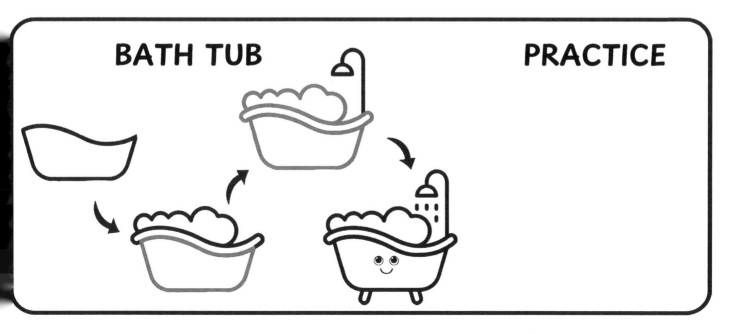

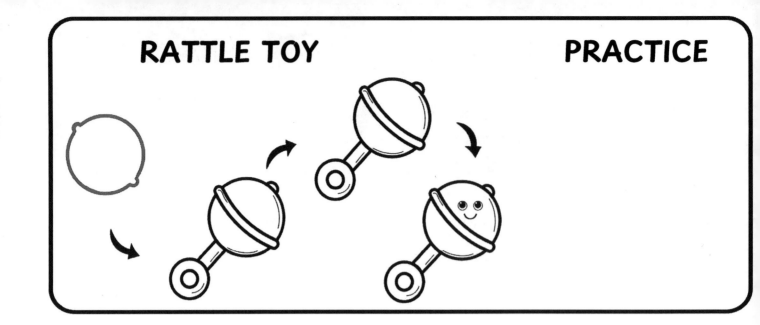

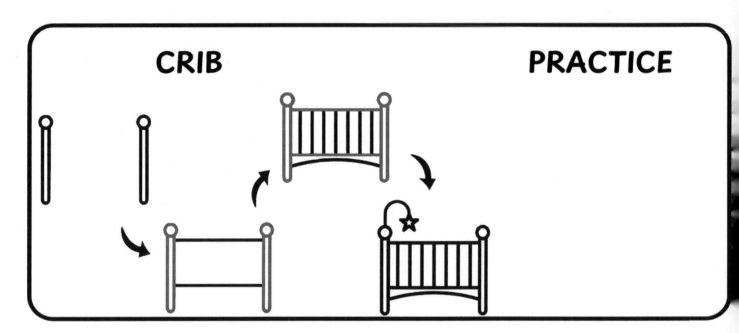

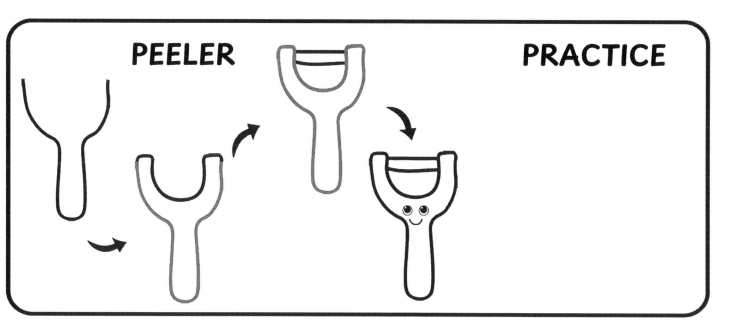
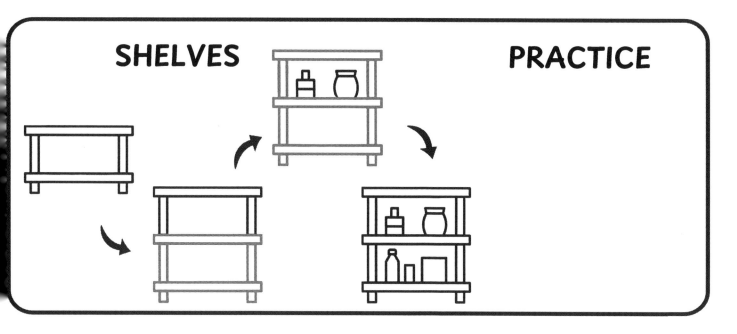
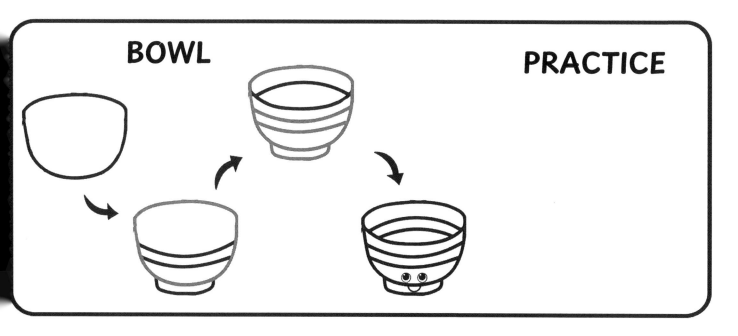

ROLLER SKATES — PRACTICE

FRAME — PRACTICE

MARKERS — PRACTICE

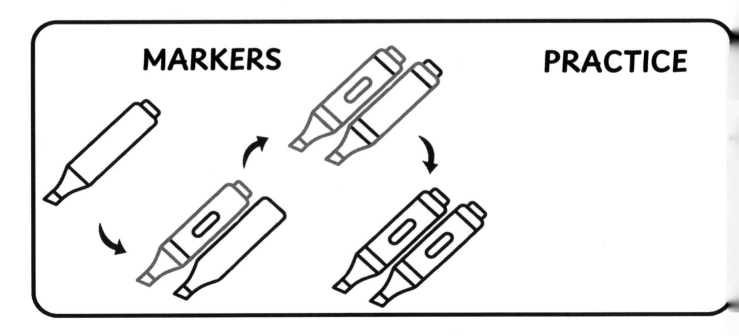

TRAFFIC LIGHTS — PRACTICE

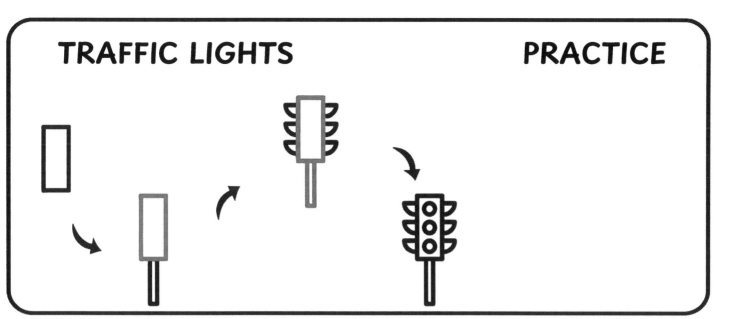

BATH TUB — PRACTICE

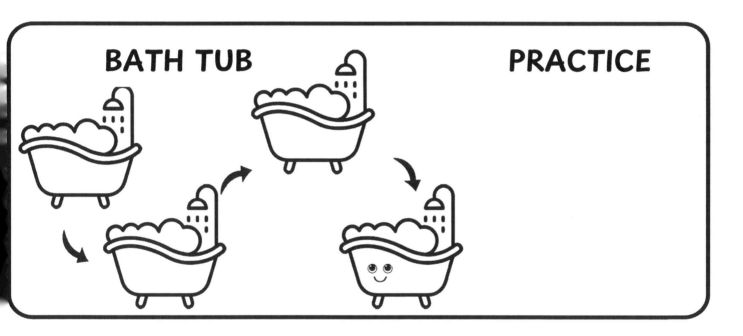

SAND BUCKET — PRACTICE

FRAME PRACTICE

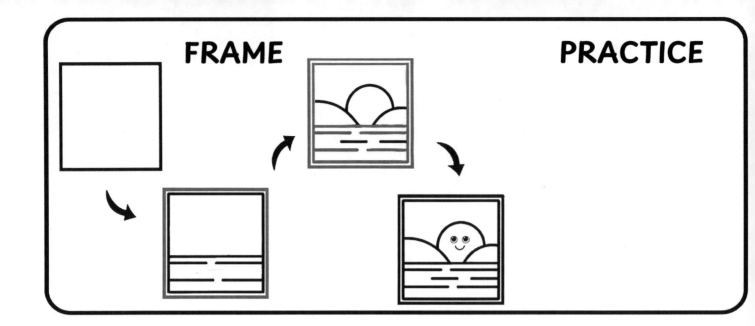

COCONUT PRACTICE

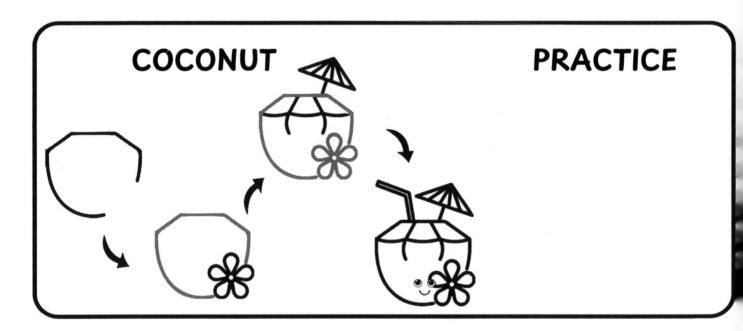

TRAVEL BAG PRACTICE

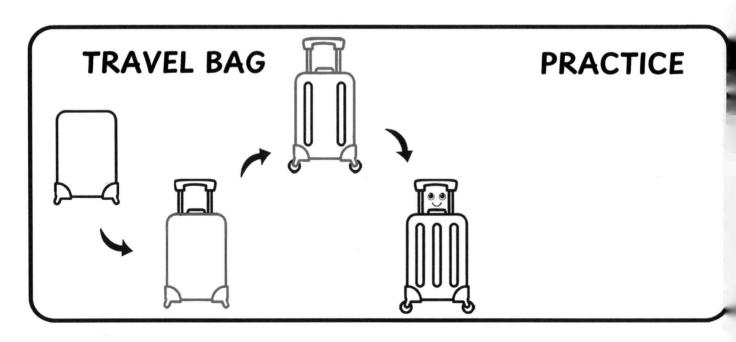

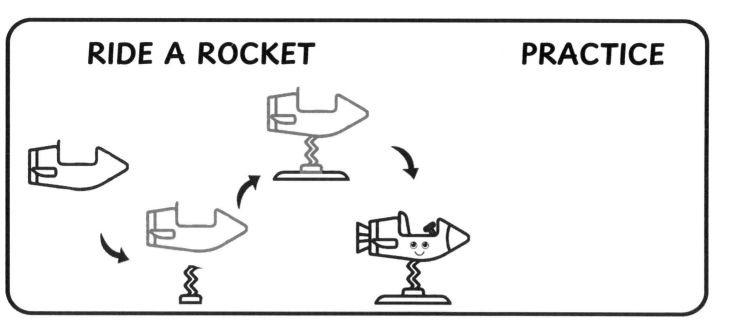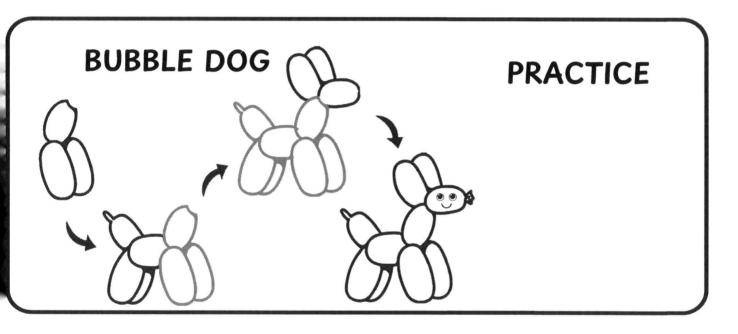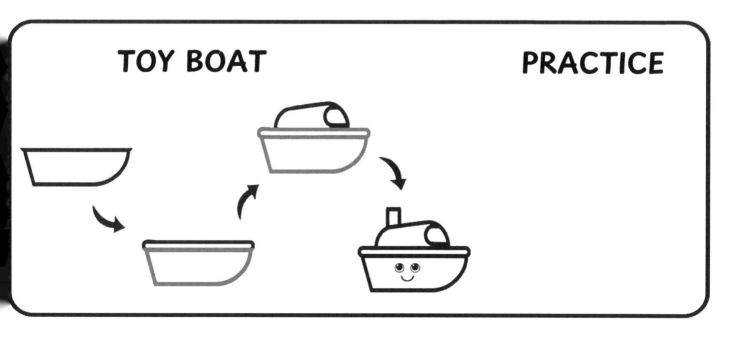

SWEET TOY — PRACTICE

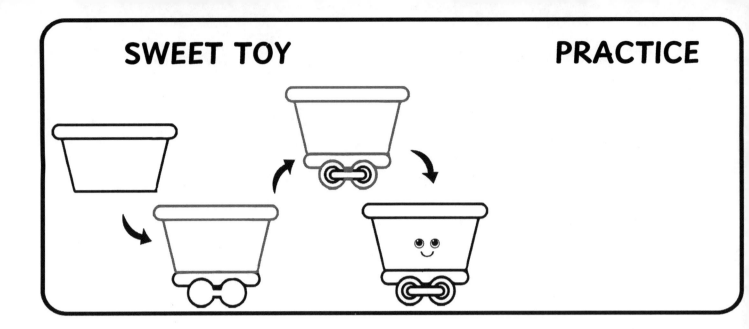

CANDIES — PRACTICE

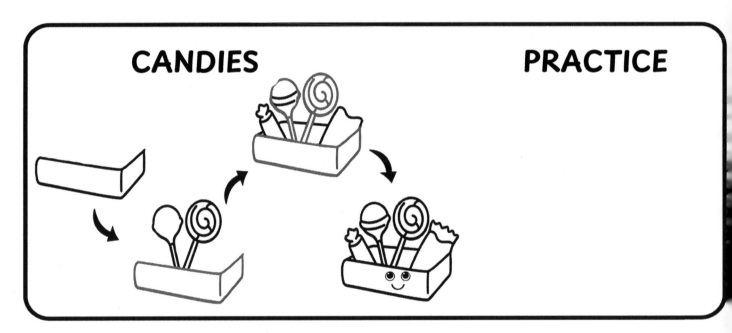

TOY BOAT — PRACTICE

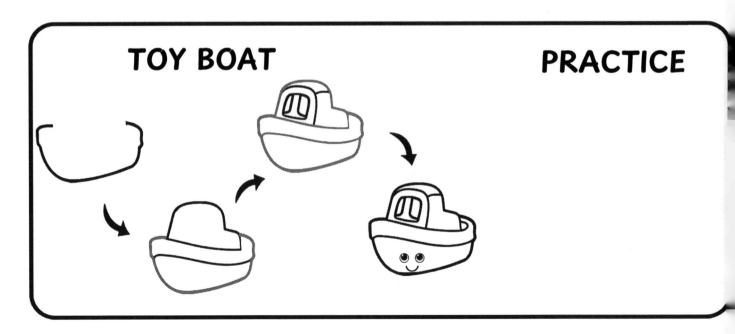

SCISSORS PRACTICE

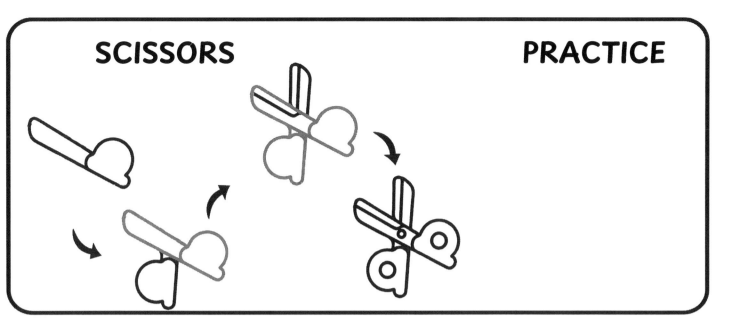

BUSINESS PRACTICE

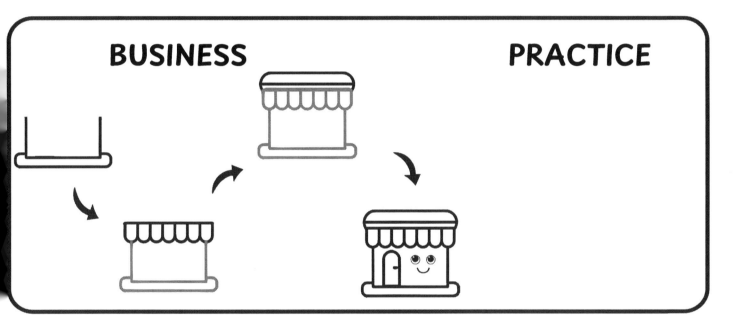

BAG PRACTICE

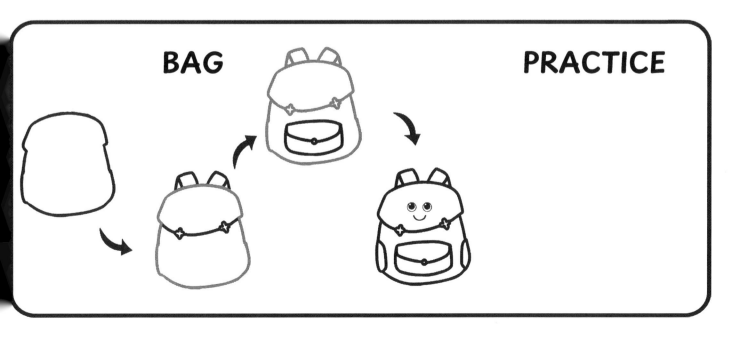

SLIPPERS — PRACTICE

PUZZLE — PRACTICE

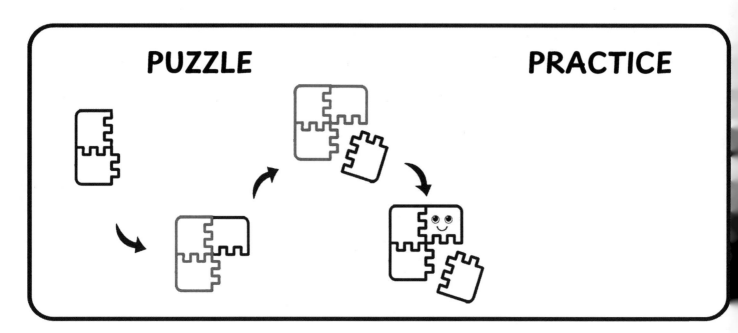

FRAME — PRACTICE

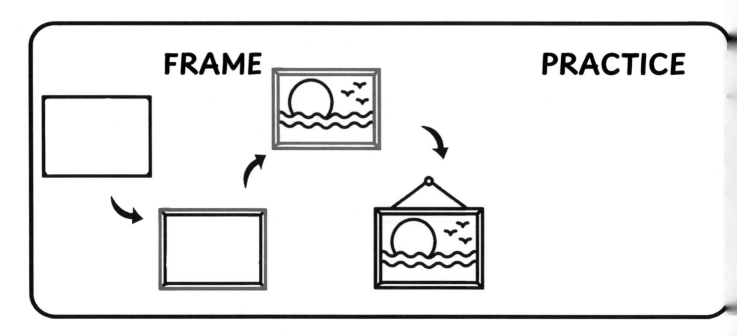

TRUMPET — PRACTICE

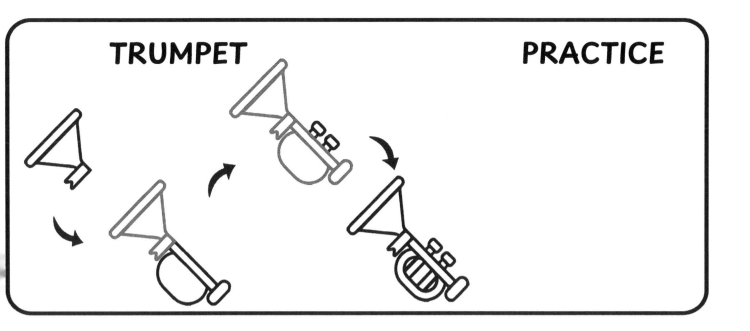

MUSHROOM HOUSE — PRACTICE

KID'S STOOL — PRACTICE

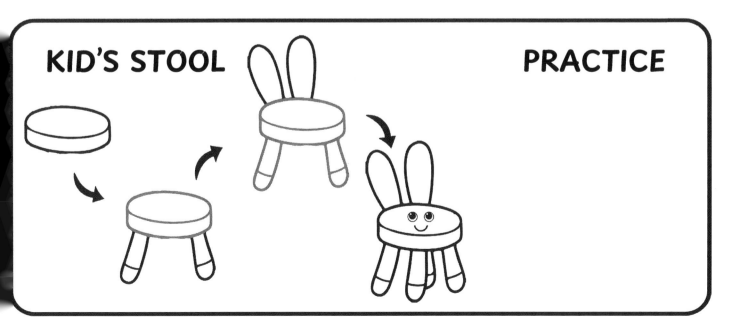

PAINT BRUSH PRACTICE

PALETE PRACTICE

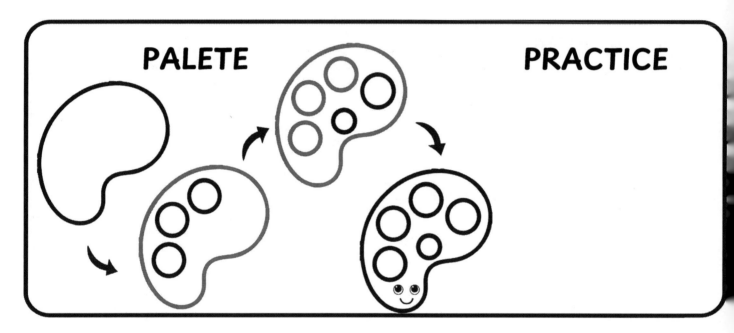

PAINTING BOARD PRACTICE

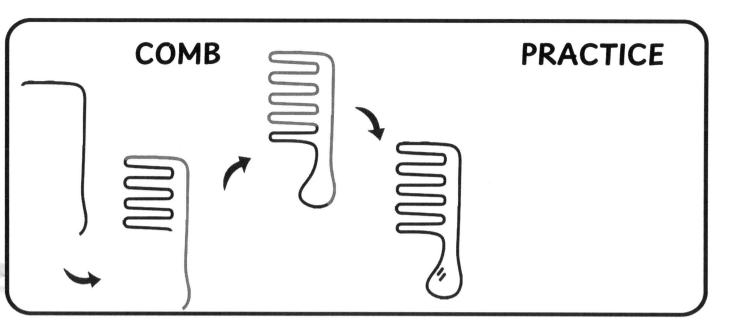
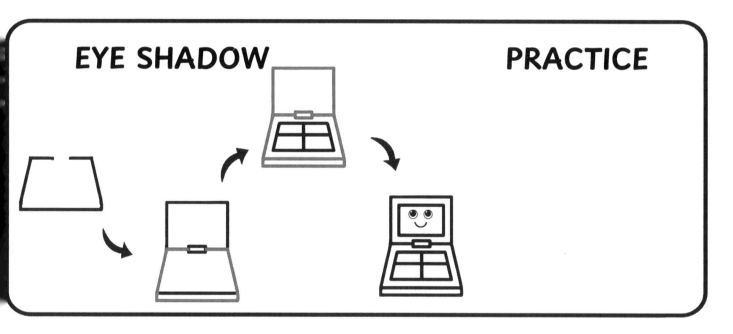
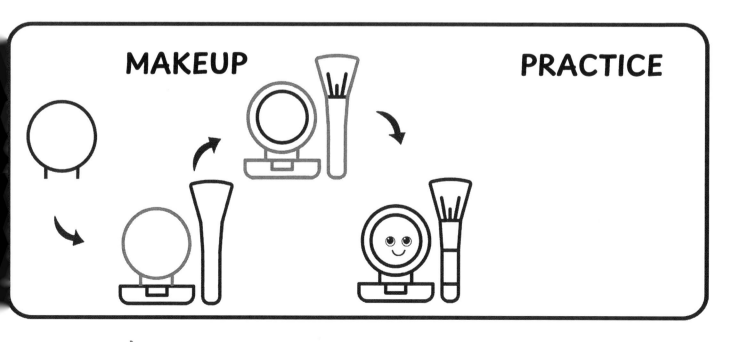

SANTA CLAUS PRACTICE

WINTER TREE PRACTICE
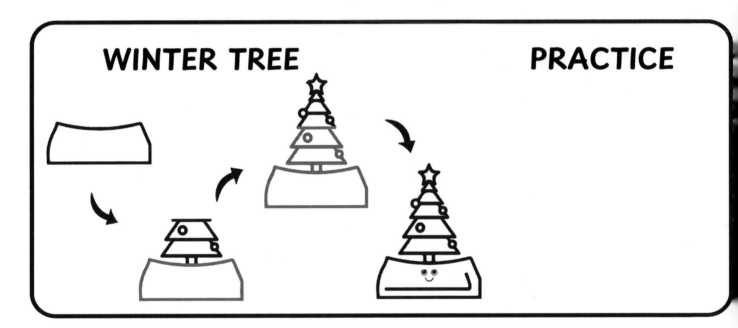

SNOW MAN PRACTICE

PANT PRACTICE

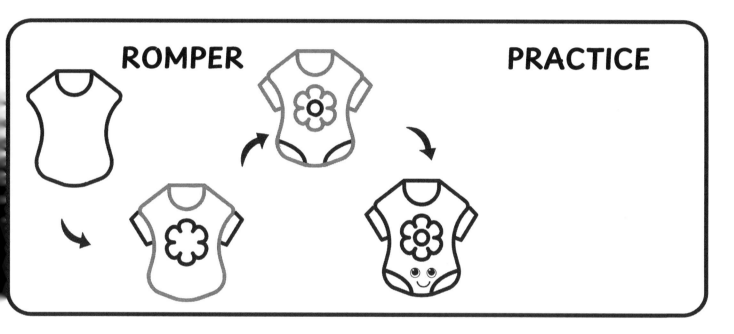

ROMPER PRACTICE

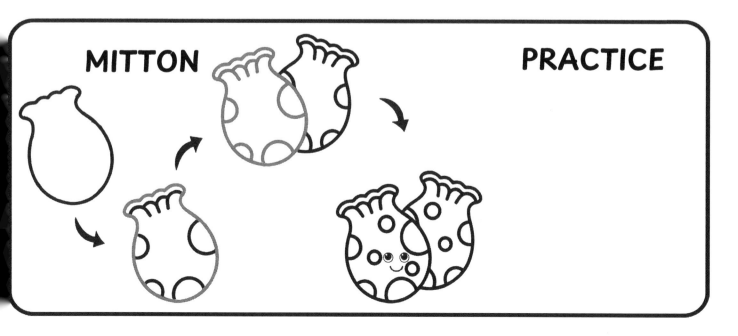

MITTON PRACTICE

ABACUS PRACTICE

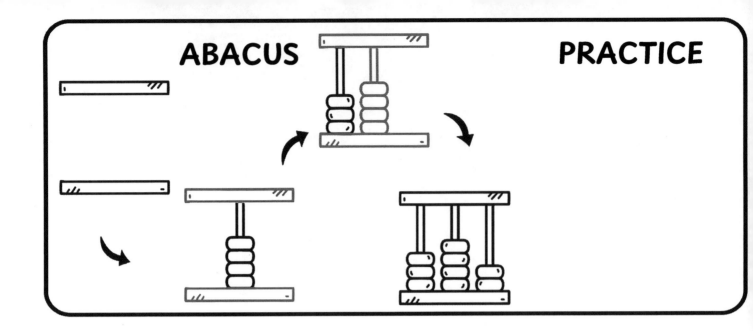

SPINNING TOP PRACTICE

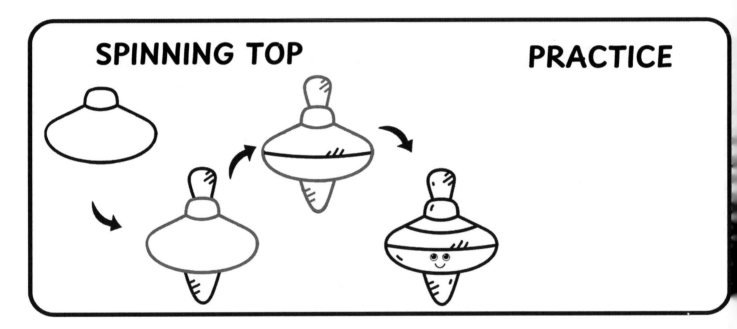

ART PRACTICE

JWELLERY PRACTICE

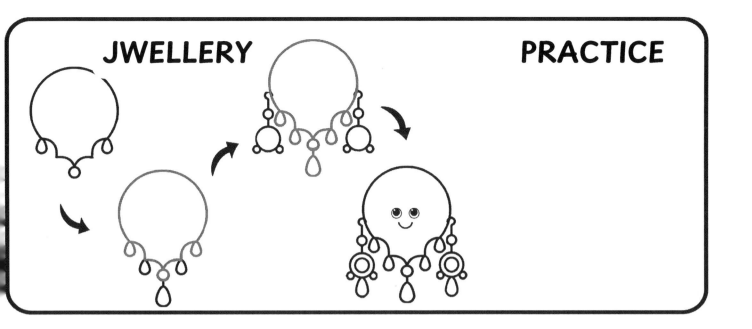

SERUM PRACTICE

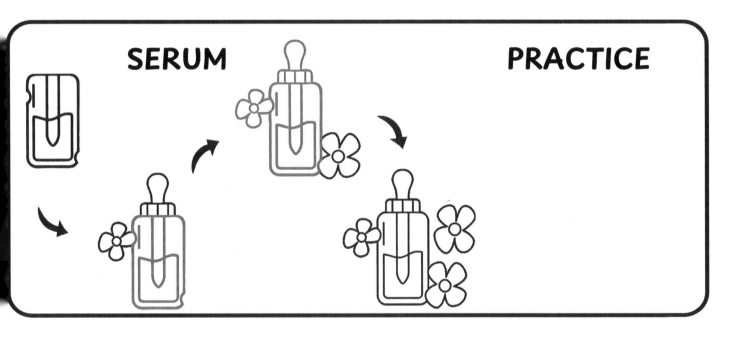

GLASS POWDER PRACTICE

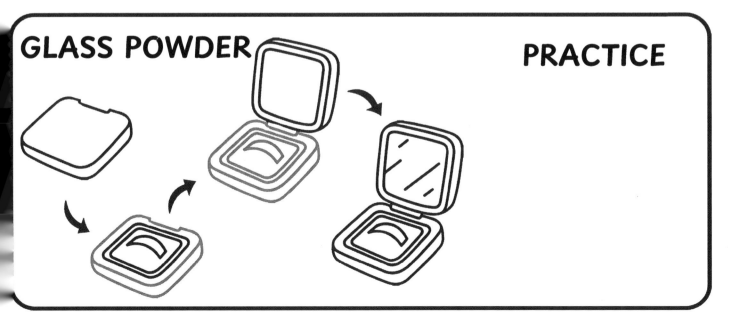

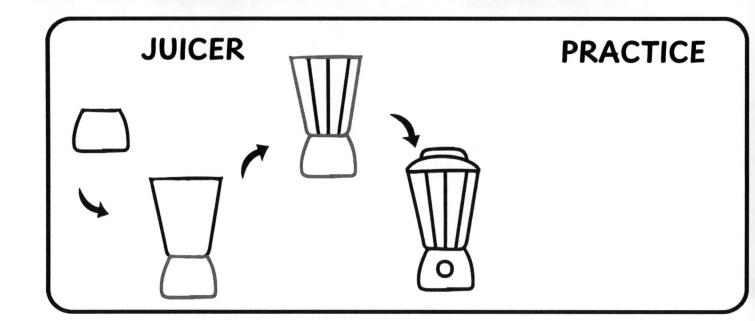
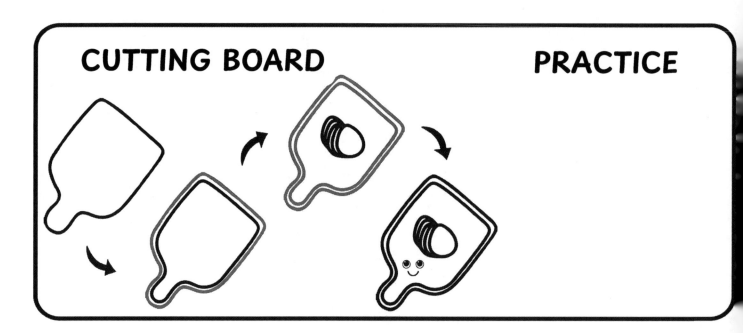

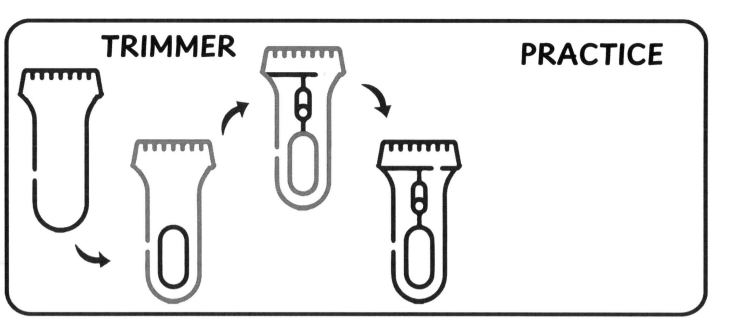
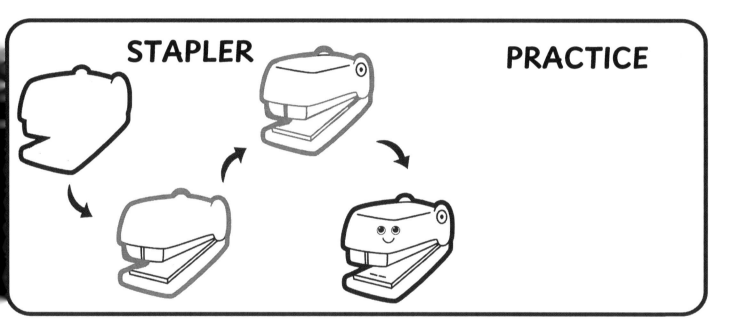
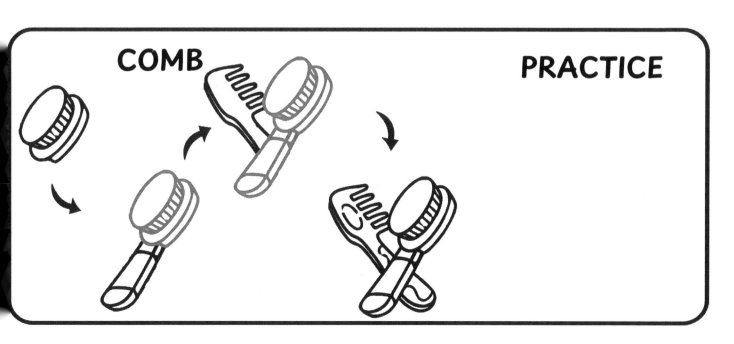

BALL PRACTICE

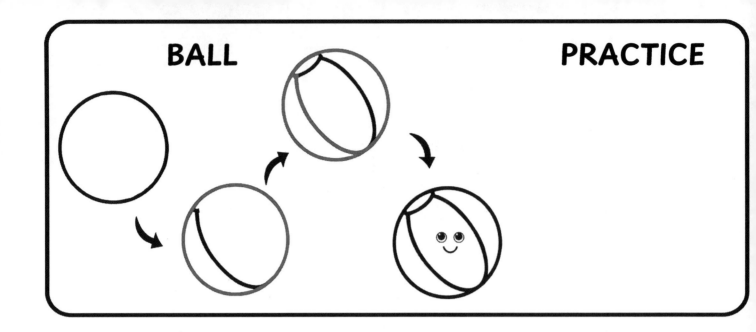

WASHING MACHINE PRACTICE

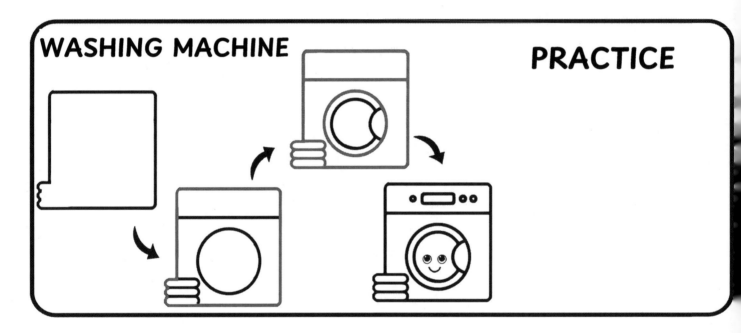

PIANO PRACTICE

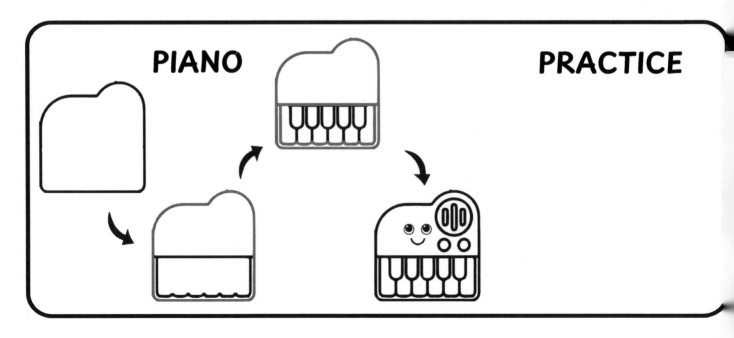

Chapter 2: Animals and Birds

PARROT
PRACTICE

OWL
PRACTICE

LION
PRACTICE

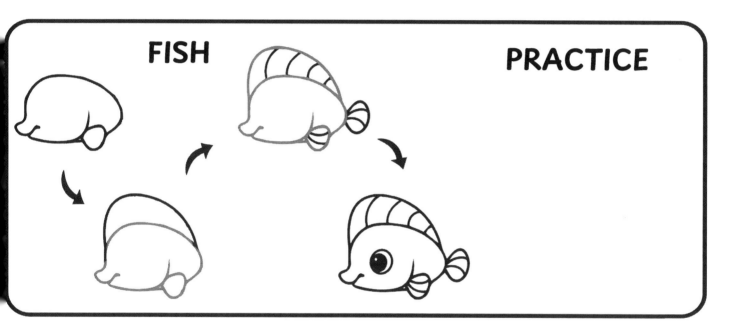

FROG PRACTICE

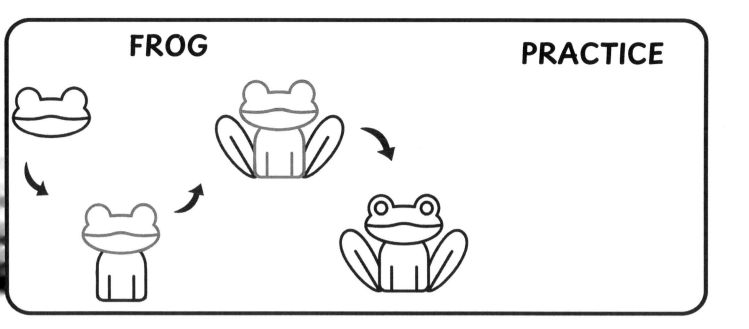

HORSE PRACTICE

SNAIL PRACTICE

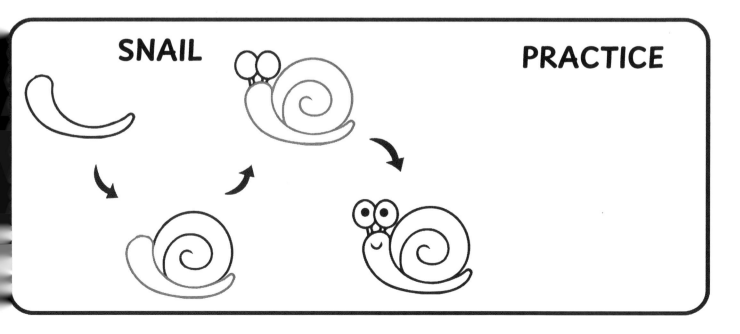

APE PRACTICE

JELLY FISH PRACTICE

TORTOISE PRACTICE

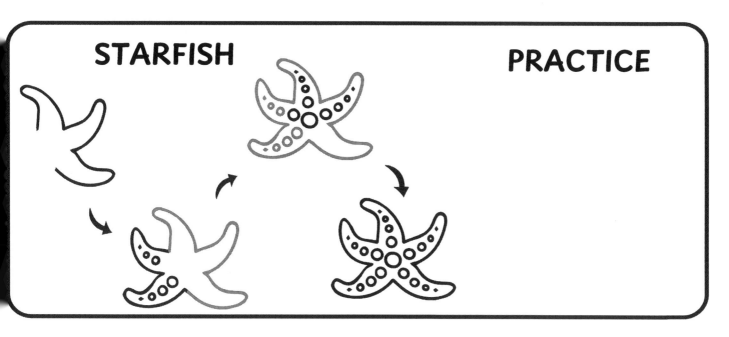

SHEEP PRACTICE

DUCK PRACTICE

HAWK PRACTICE

WALRUS PRACTICE

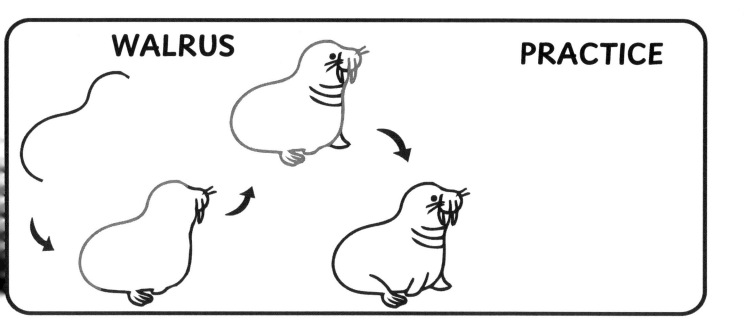

RACOON PRACTICE

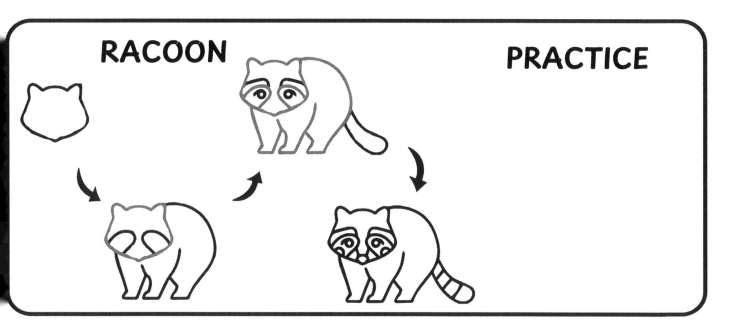

LIZARD PRACTICE

DOG PRACTICE

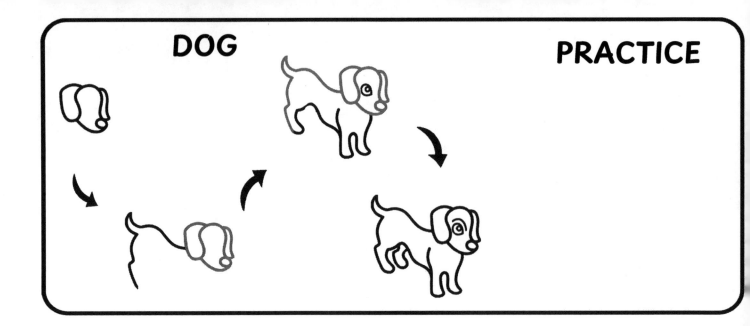

GORILLA PRACTICE

LOBSTER PRACTICE

SQUID PRACTICE

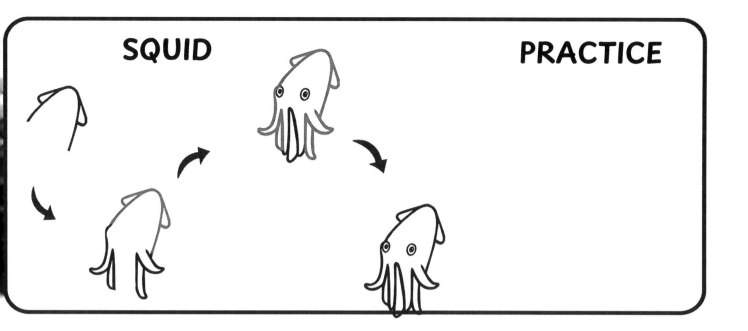

COW PRACTICE

CROW PRACTICE

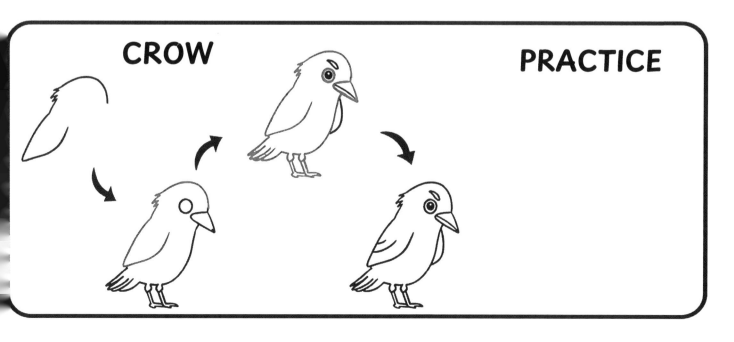

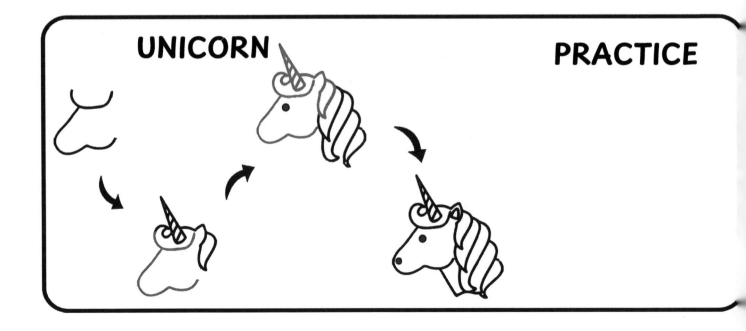

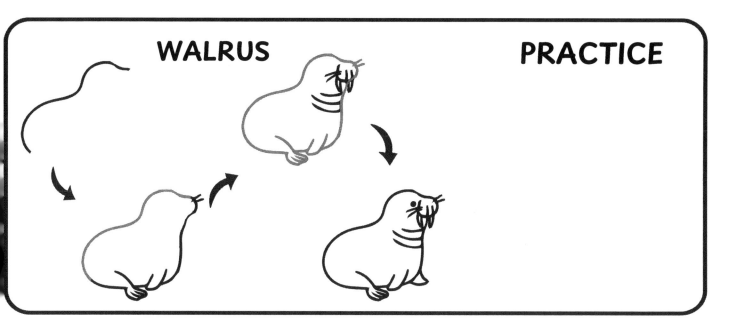
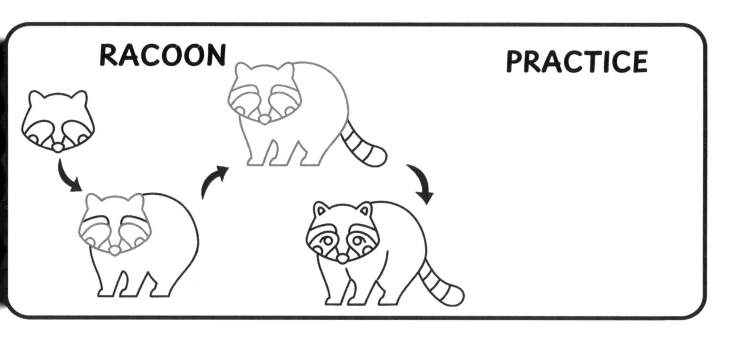

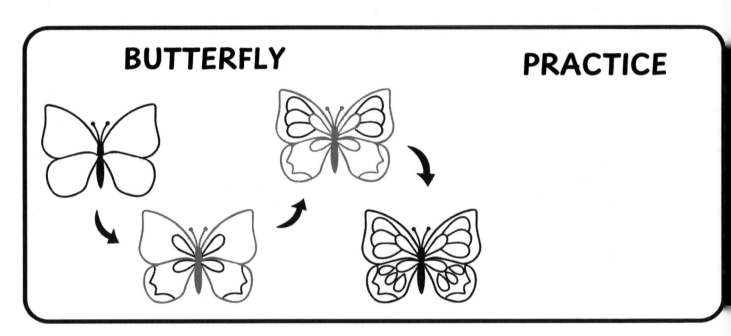

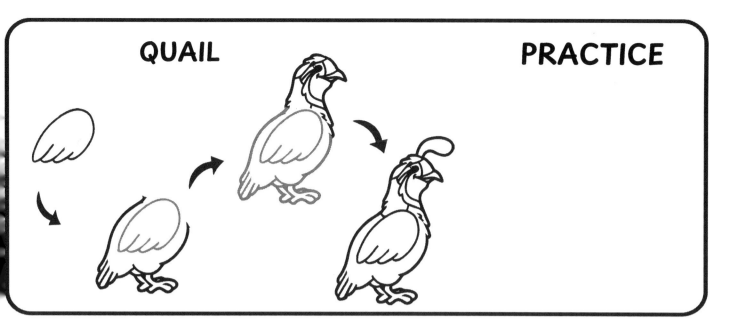

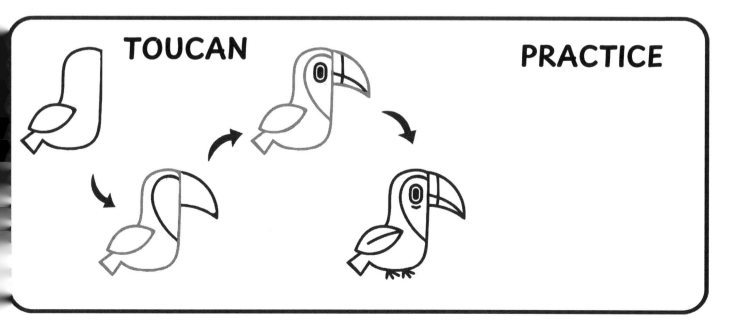

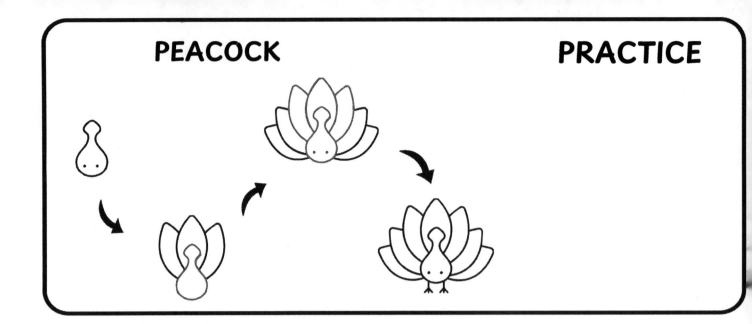

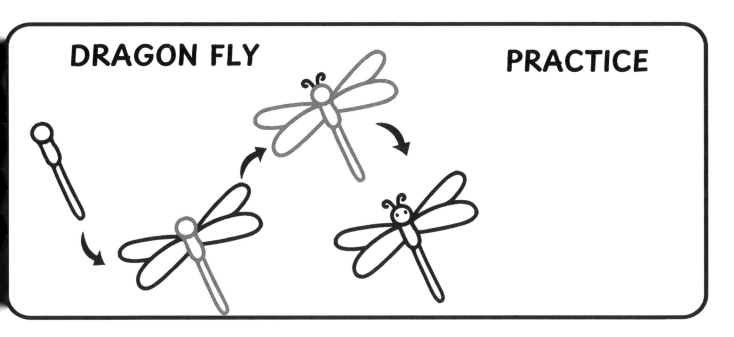
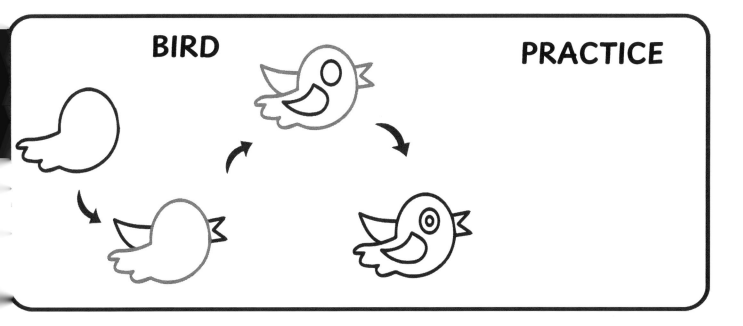

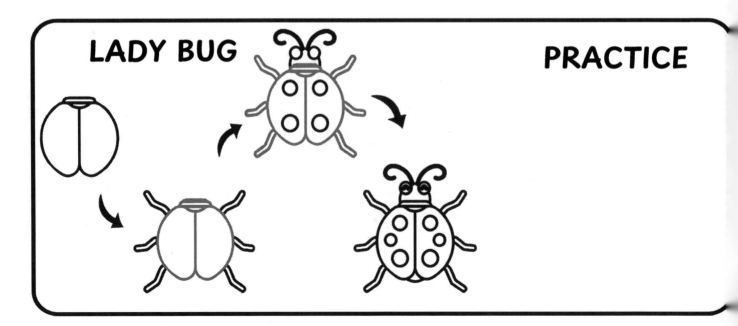

Chapter 3: Food and Drink

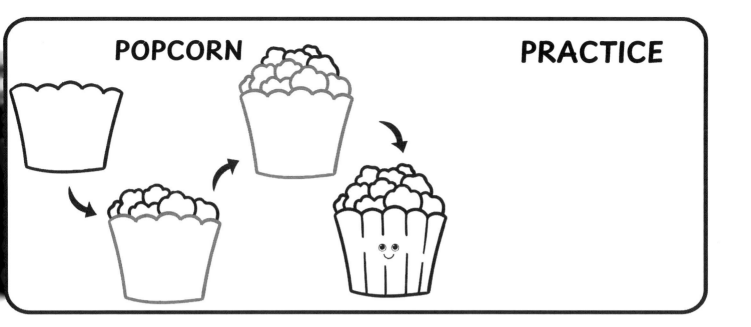
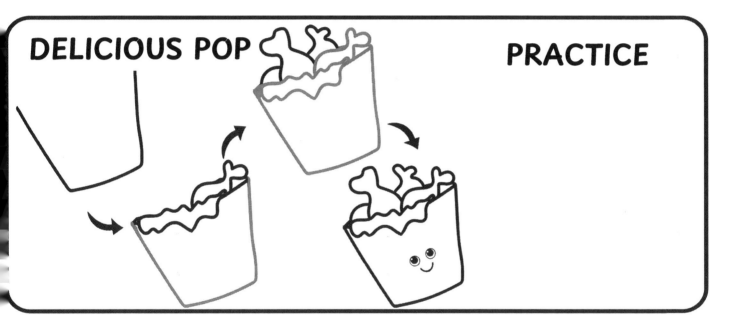

ICE CREAM — PRACTICE

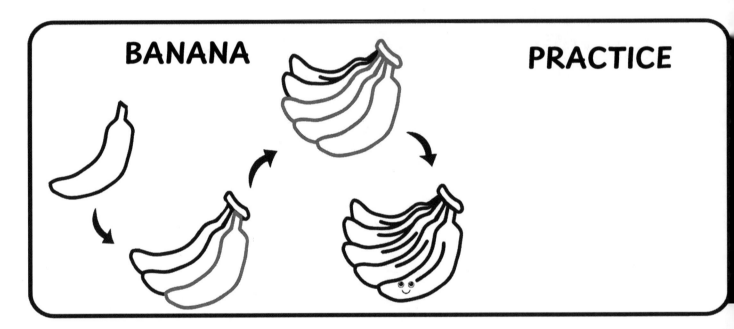

BANANA — PRACTICE

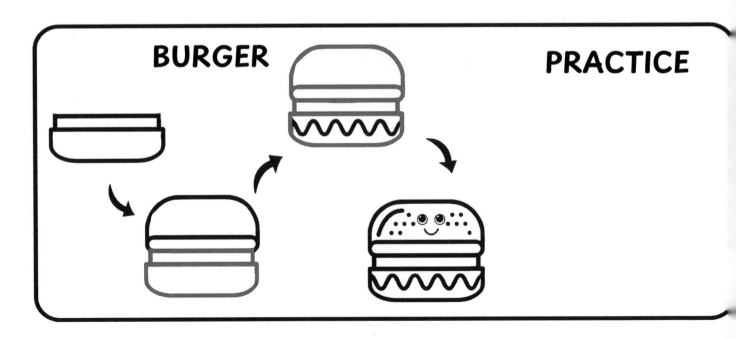

BURGER — PRACTICE

WATERMELON PRACTICE

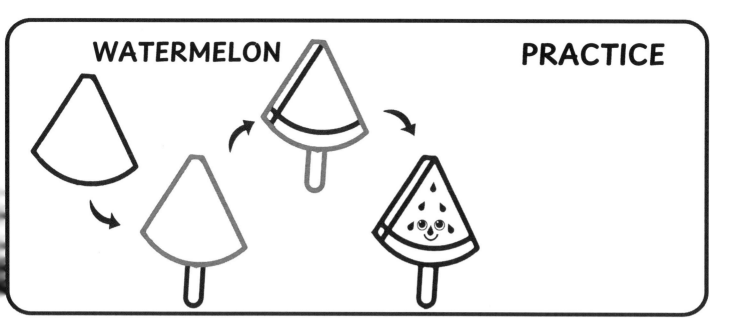

PIZZA PRACTICE

CAKE PRACTICE

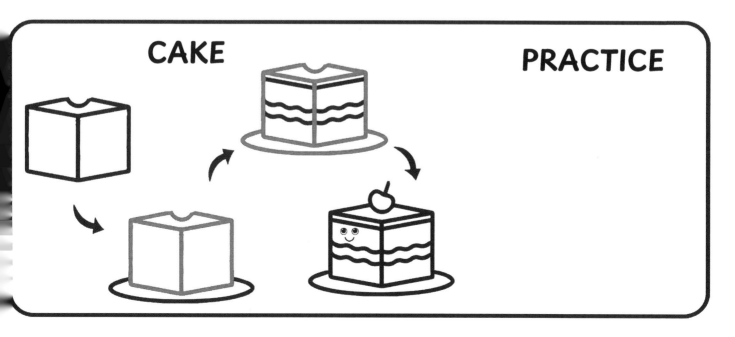

COCONUT PRACTICE

JELLY PRACTICE

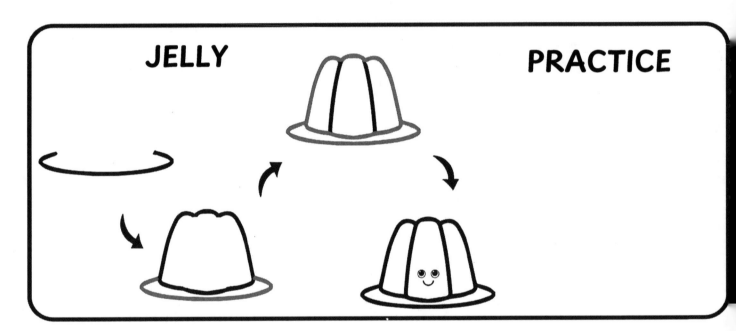

CUP-CAKE PRACTICE

COLD DRINK — PRACTICE

DANGO STICK — PRACTICE

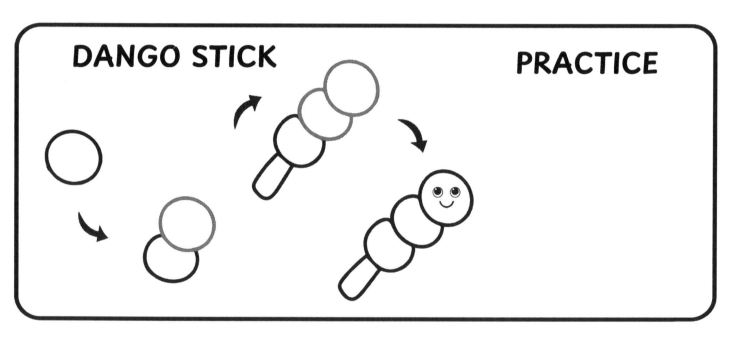

FRIES — PRACTICE

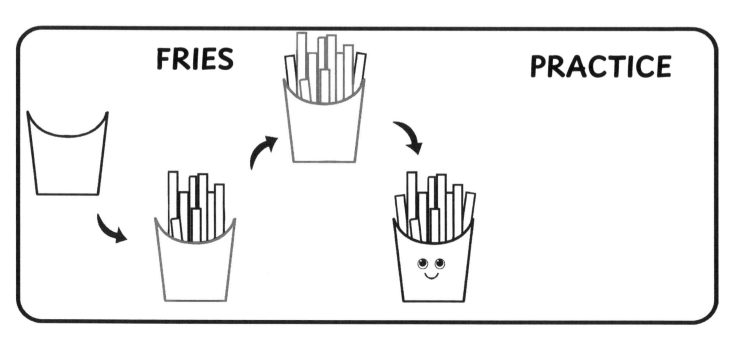

ONION PRACTICE

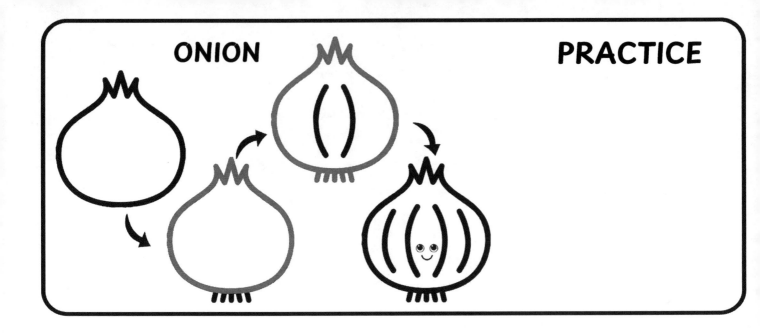

VEGETABLES PRACTICE

CEREALS PRACTICE

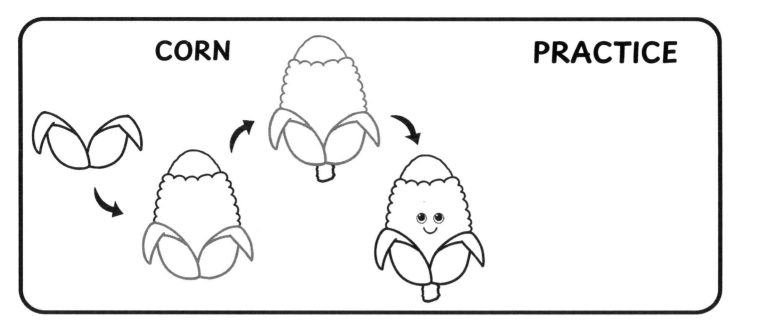

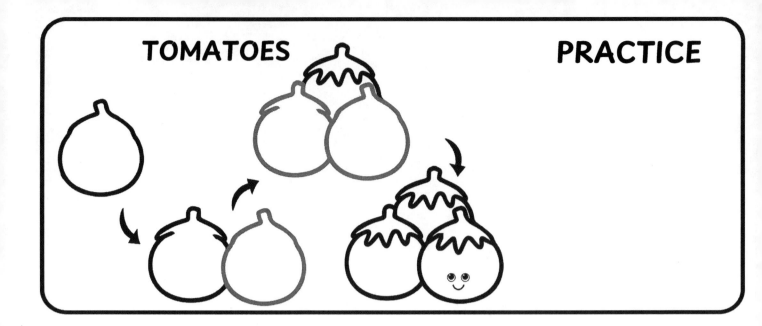
TOMATOES — PRACTICE

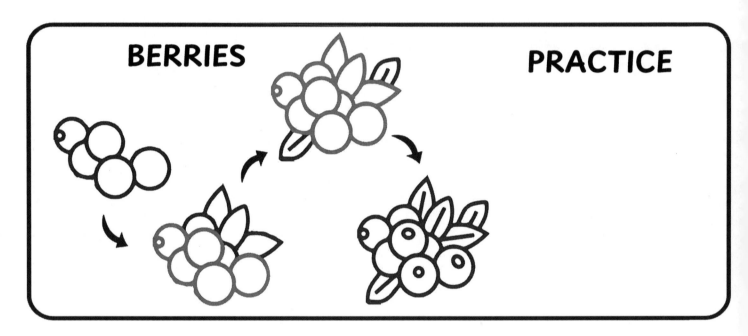
BERRIES — PRACTICE

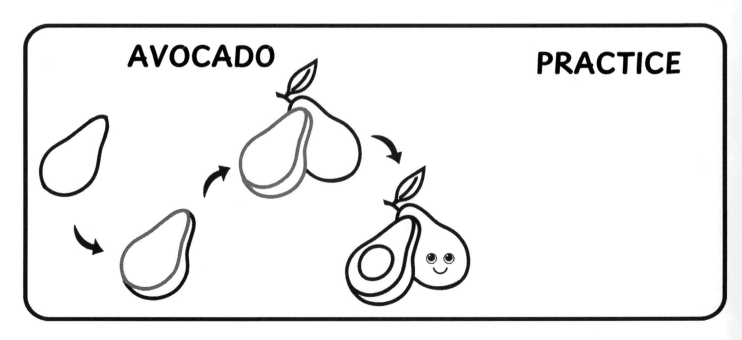
AVOCADO — PRACTICE

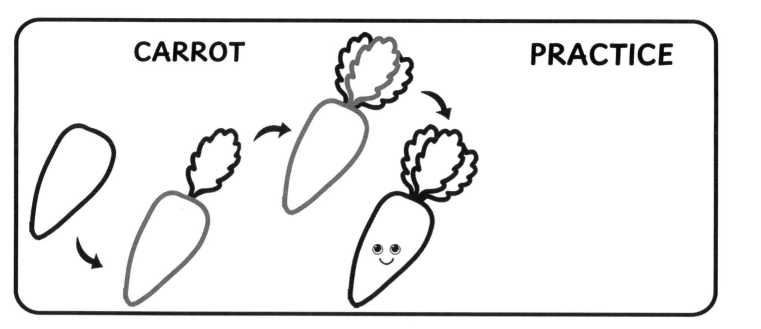

CARROT — PRACTICE

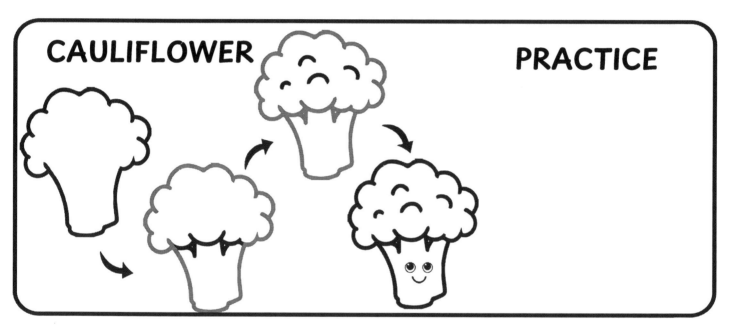

CAULIFLOWER — PRACTICE

REDDISH — PRACTICE

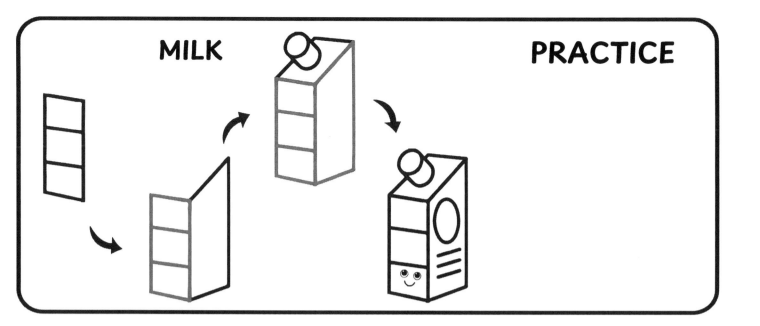

CREAM PRACTICE

ICECREAM PRACTICE

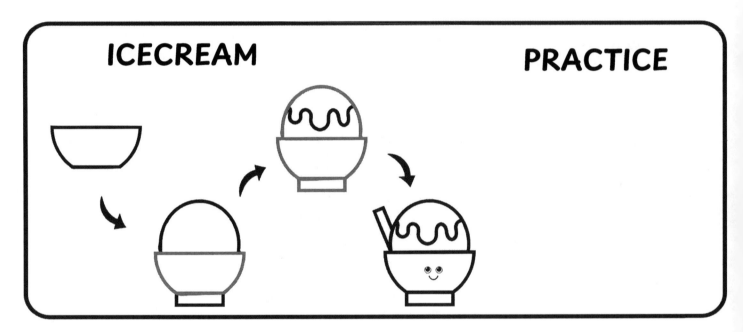

SUGAR BOWL PRACTICE

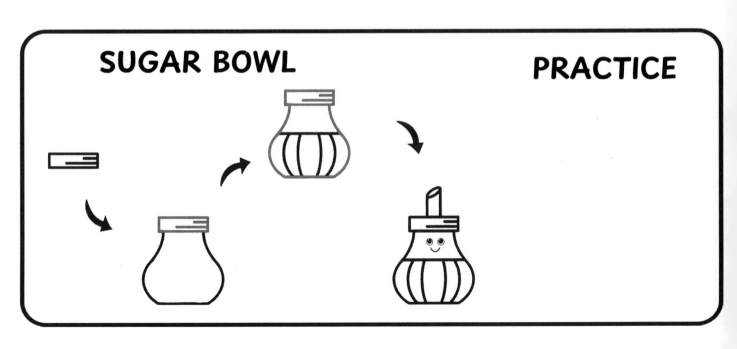

ICECREAM PRACTICE

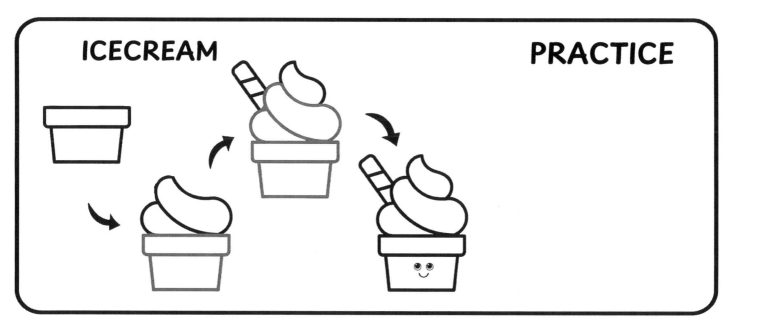

CANDY PRACTICE

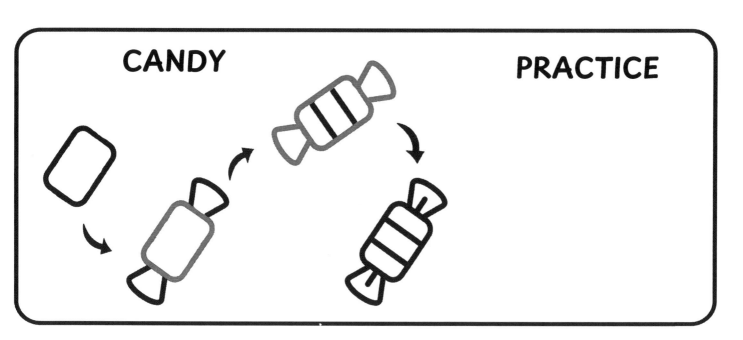

DRINK PRACTICE

SABDWICH PRACTICE

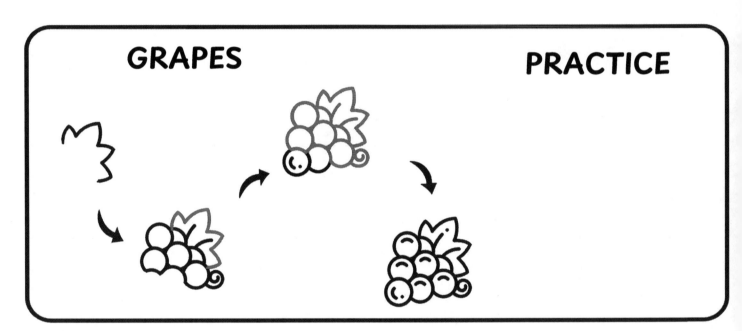

GRAPES PRACTICE

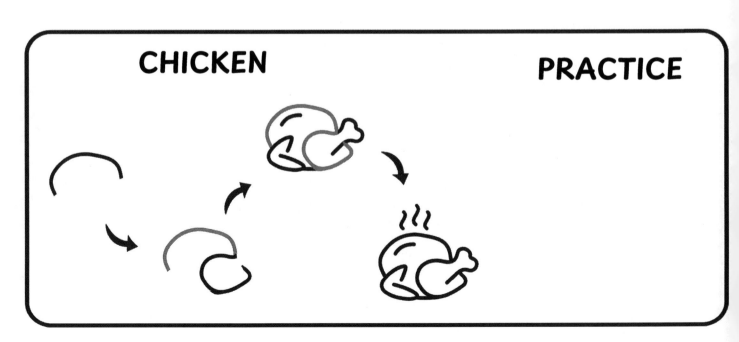

CHICKEN PRACTICE

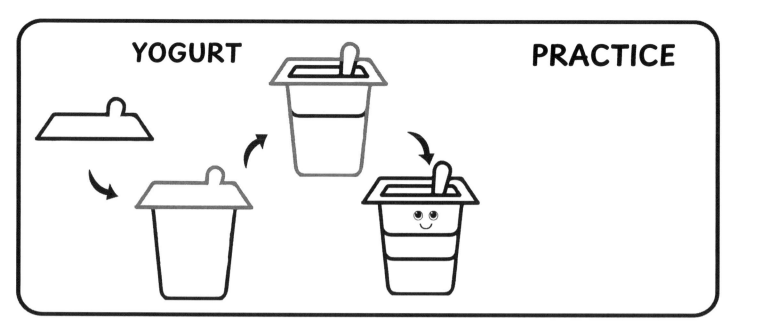
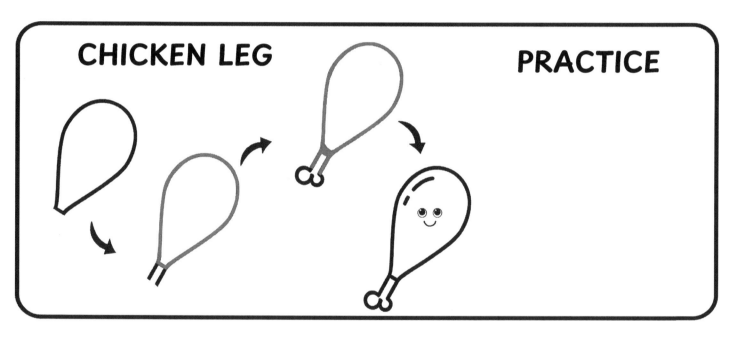
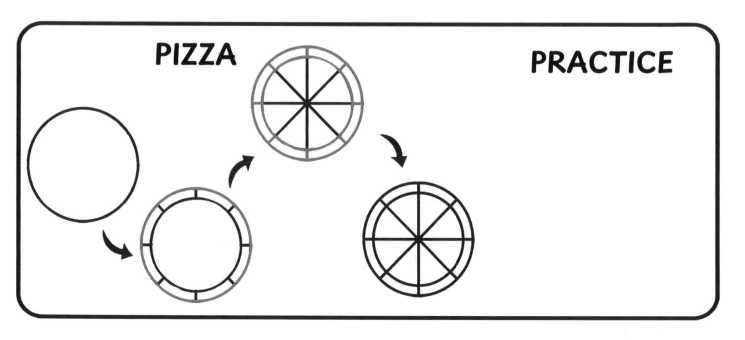

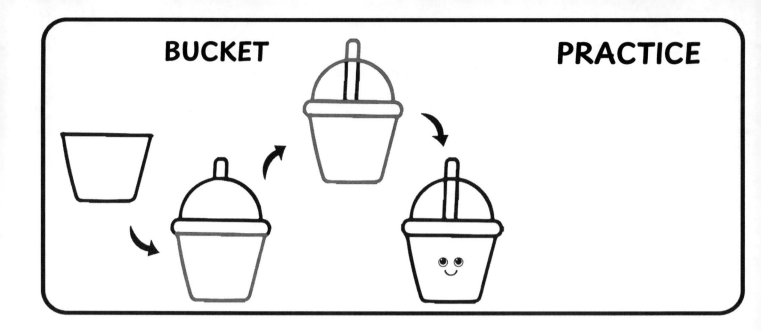
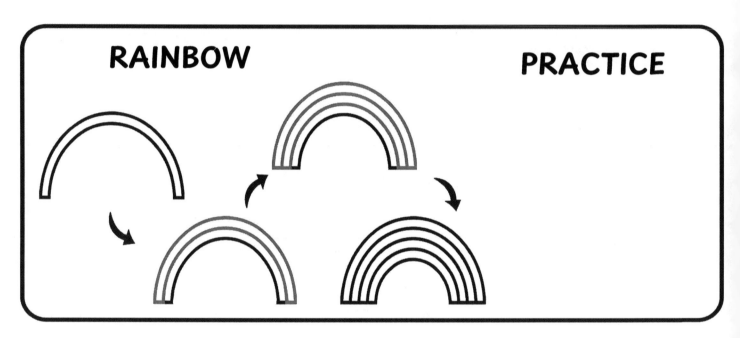

TENT PRACTICE

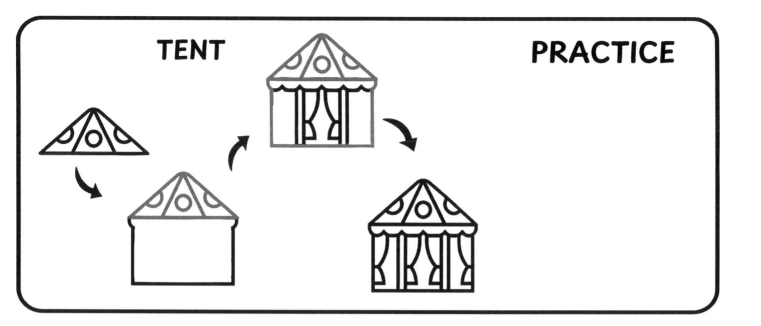

FACTORY PRACTICE

WORKERS PRACTICE

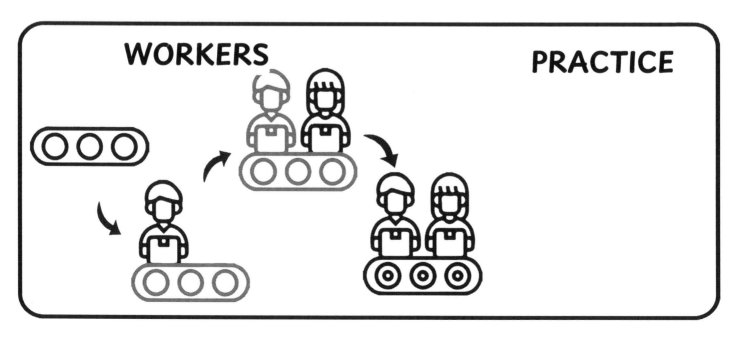

Chapter 4: Landscapes and Robots

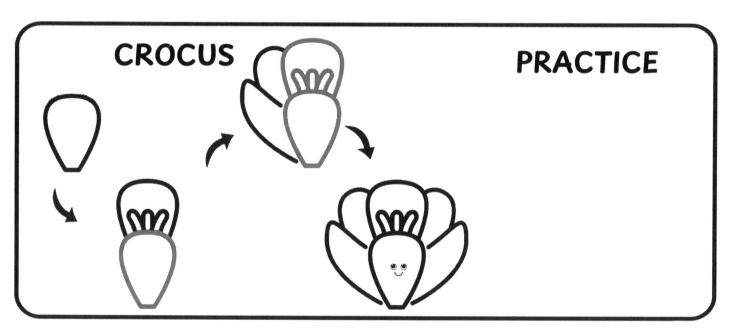
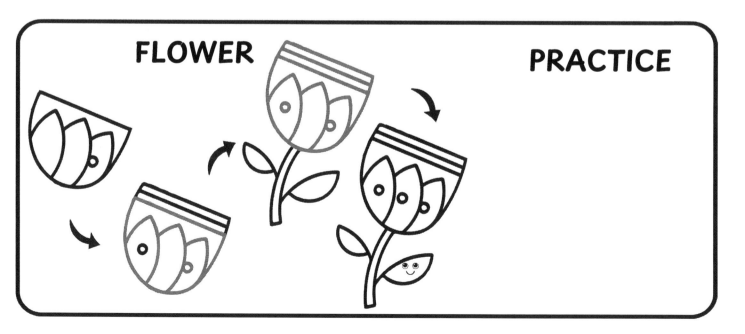

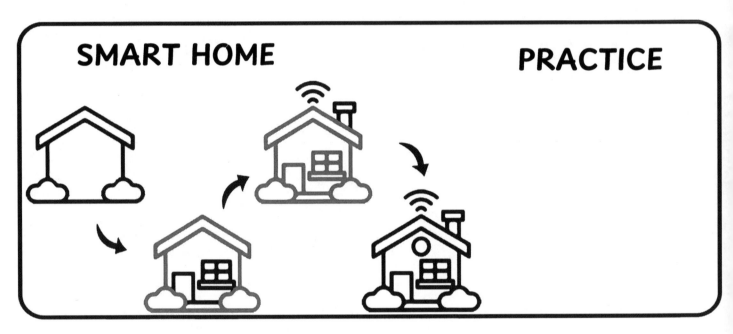

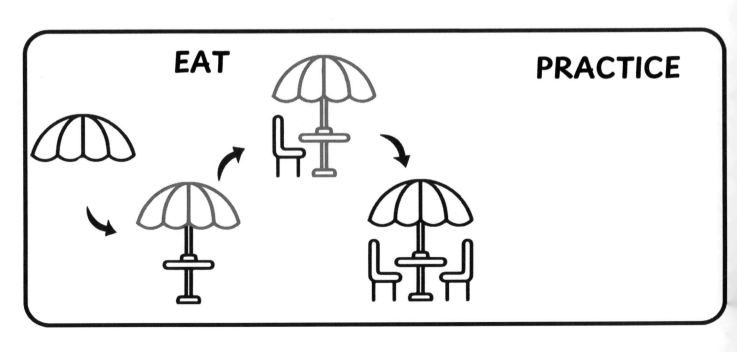

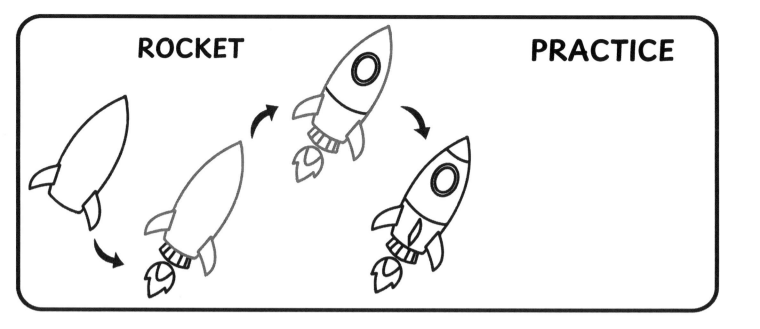

ROCKET — PRACTICE

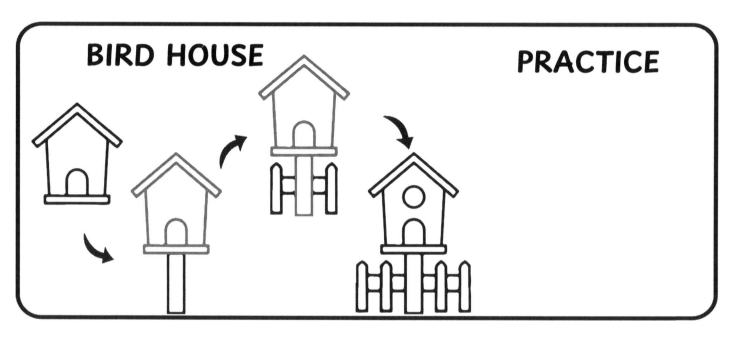

BIRD HOUSE — PRACTICE

COCONUT TREE — PRACTICE

SWEET FLOWER — PRACTICE

FLOWER BUTTON — PRACTICE

SPRING POP FLOWER — PRACTICE

NATURE PRACTICE

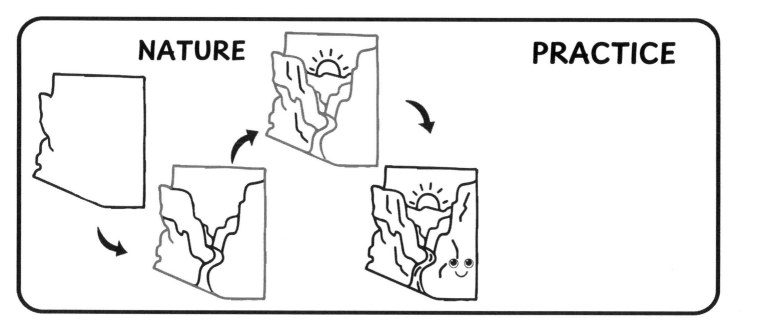

HOUSE PRACTICE

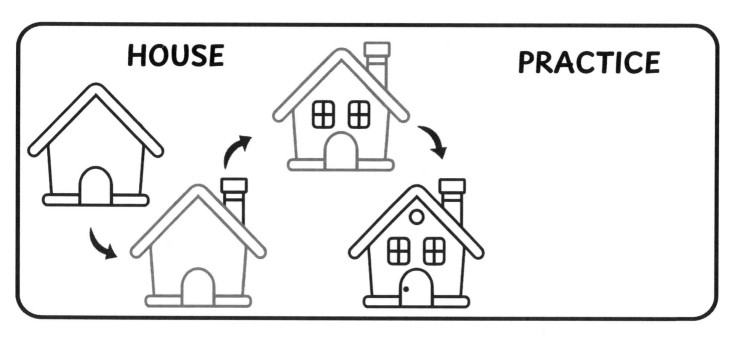

LANDSCAPE PRACTICE

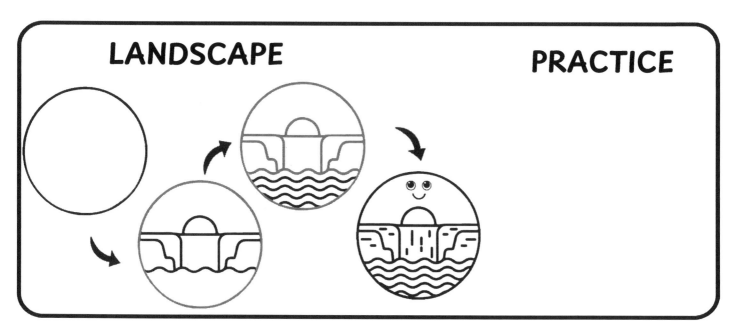

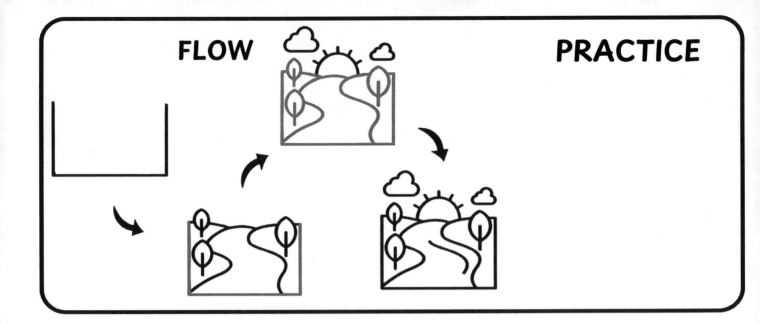
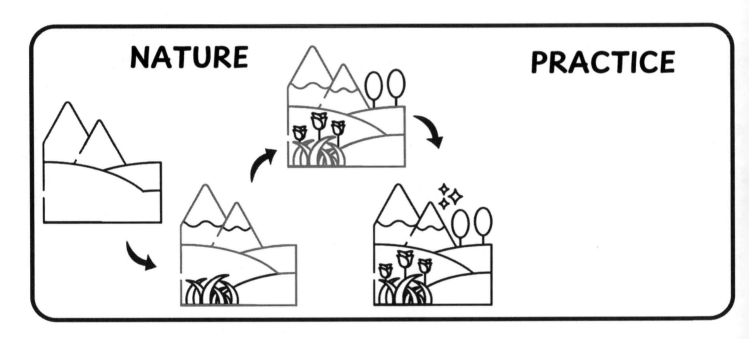

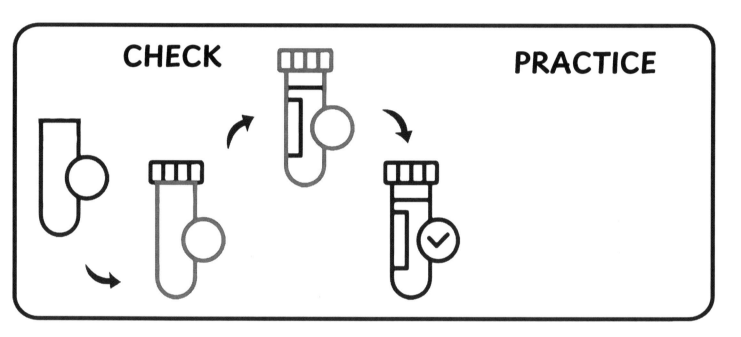
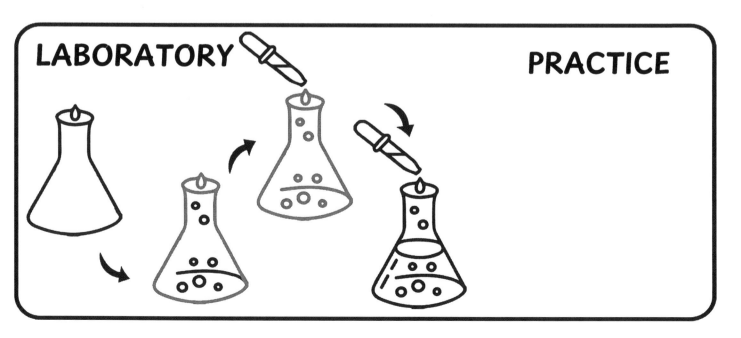

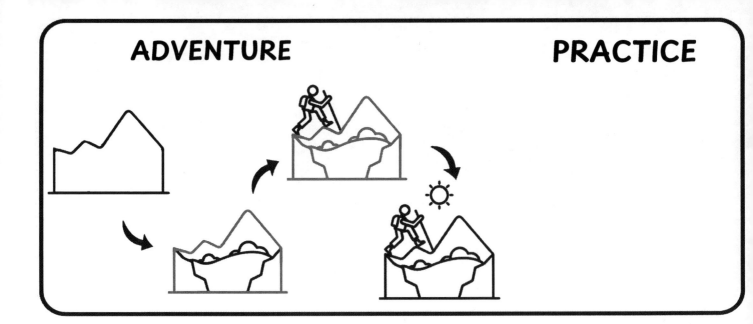
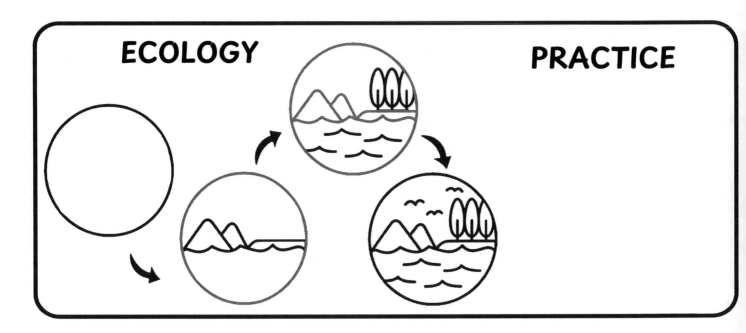
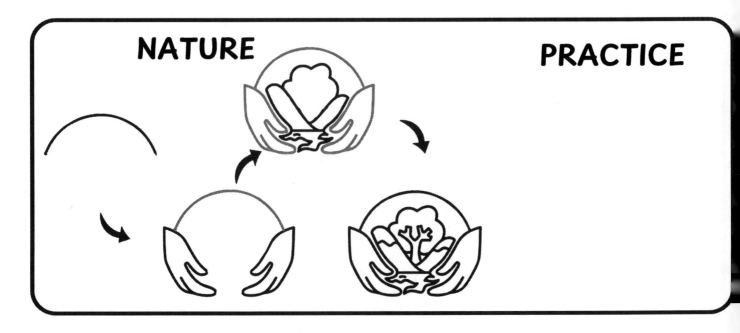

MOUNTAIN — PRACTICE

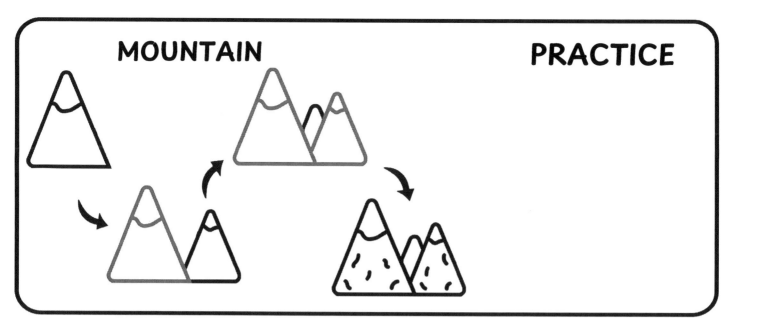

FRAME — PRACTICE

HUT — PRACTICE

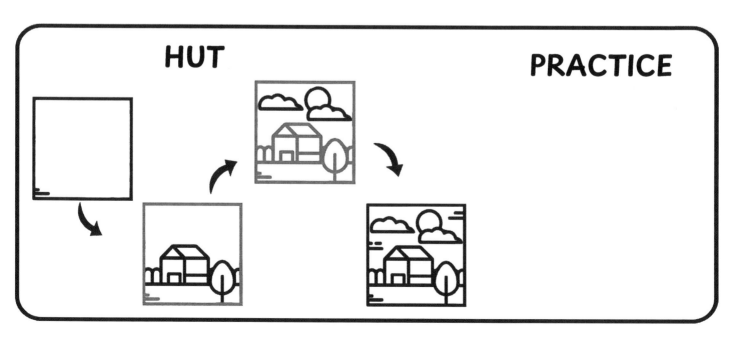

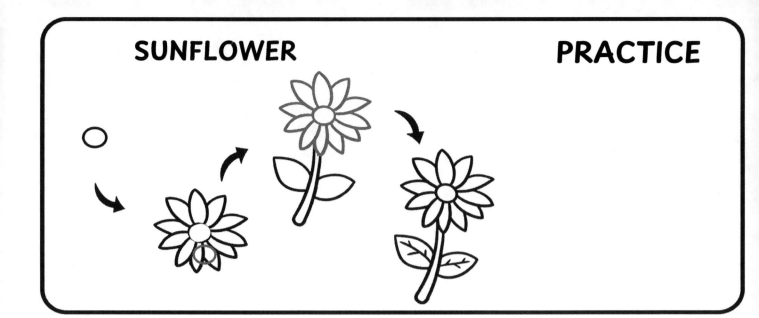

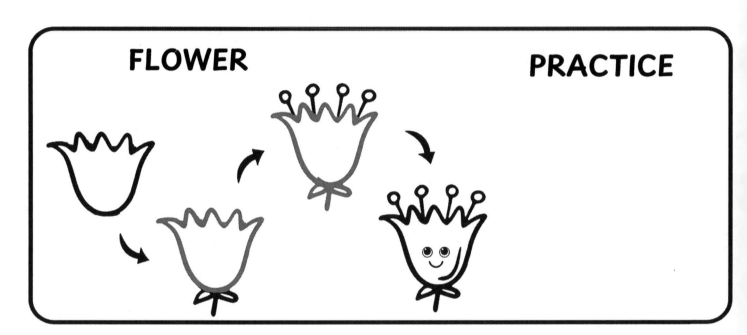

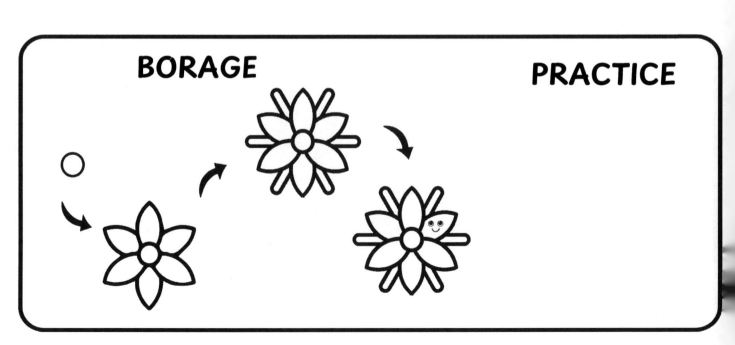

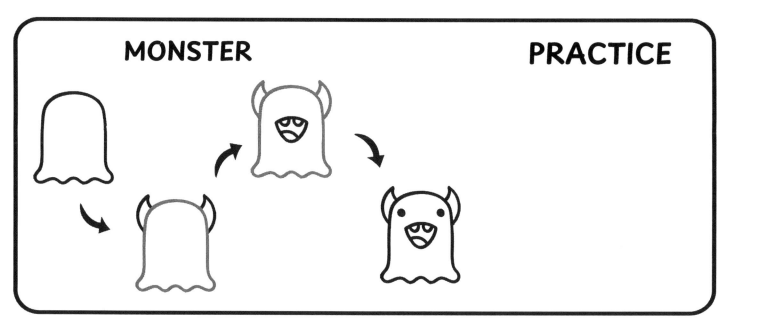

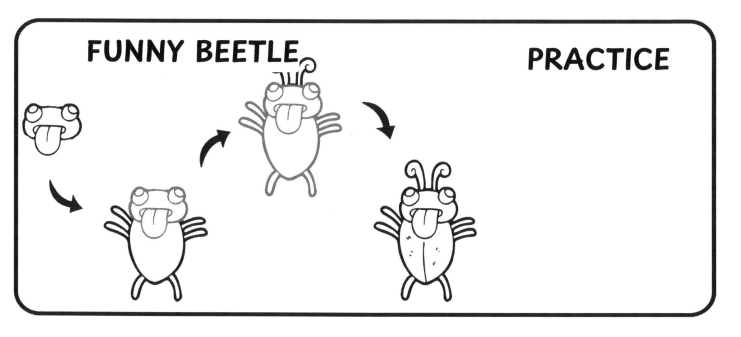

STAPLER PRACTICE

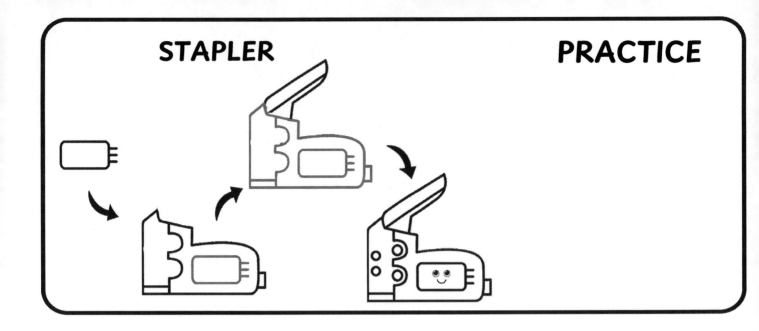

BEACH PRACTICE

STORE PRACTICE

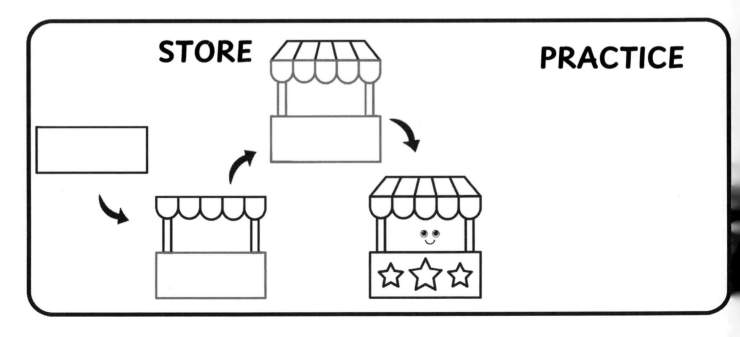

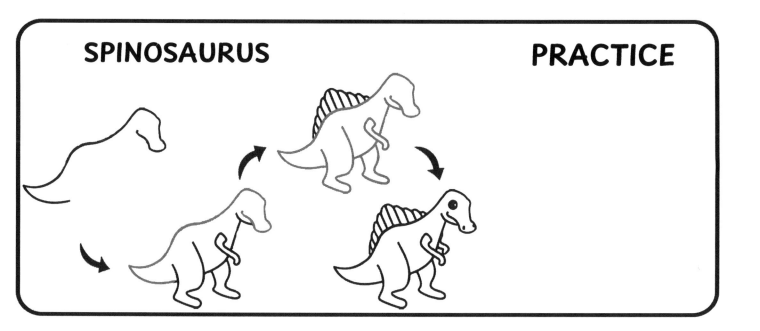

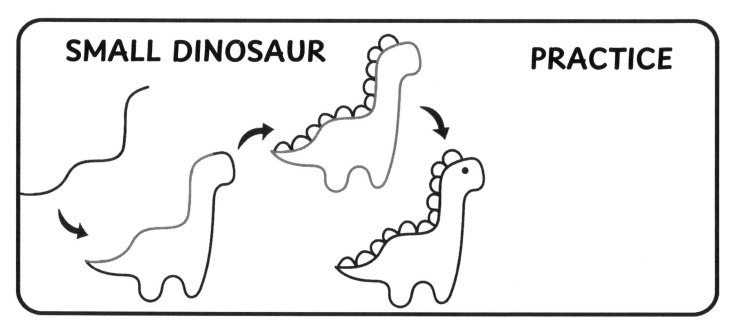

ROBOT PRACTICE

SWEET ROBOT PRACTICE

TOY CAR PRACTICE

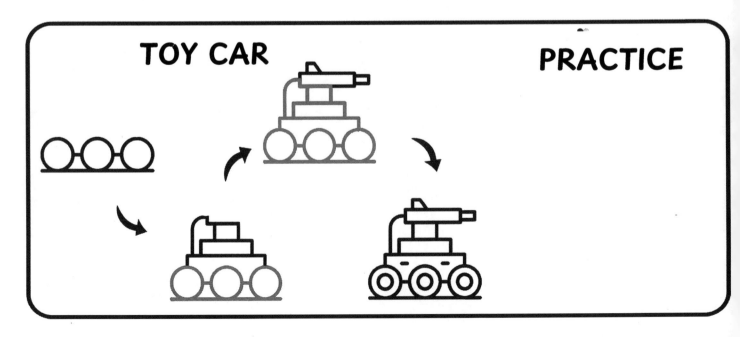

MONSTER PRACTICE

MOWING MACHINE PRACTICE

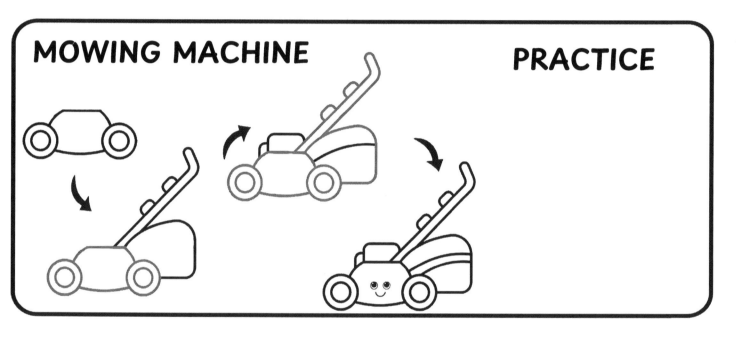

HAND ROBOT PRACTICE

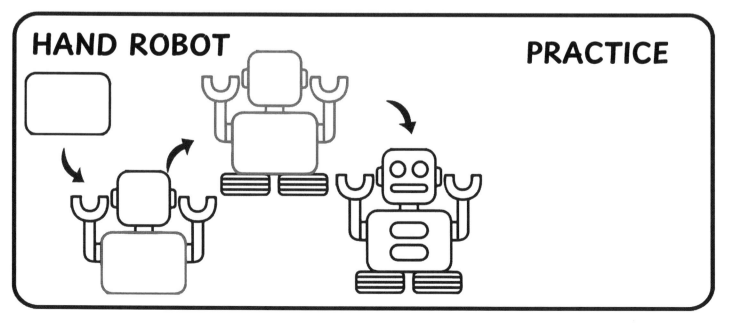

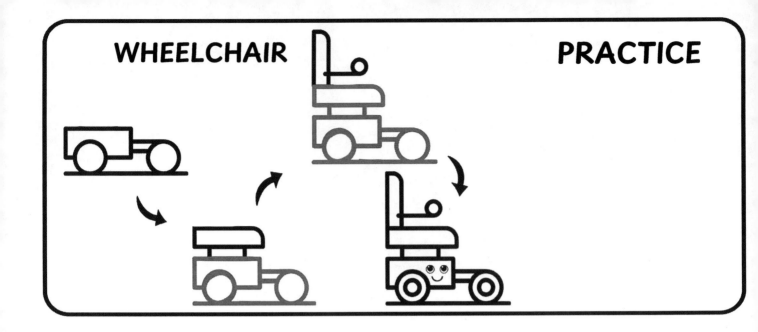
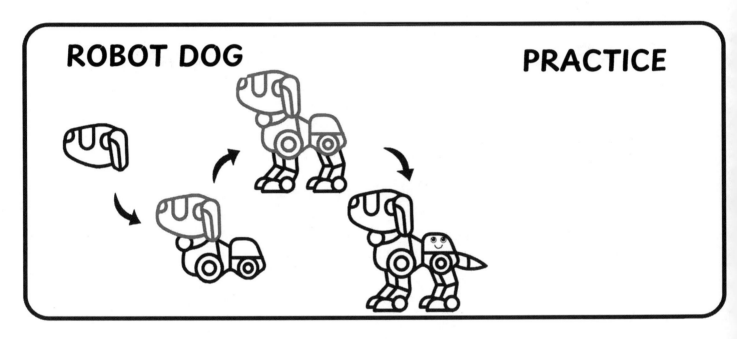
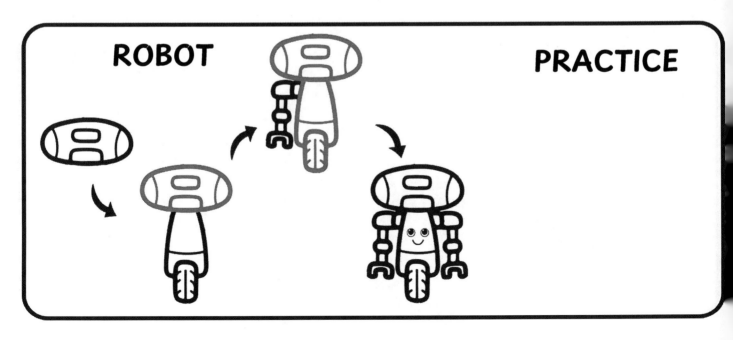

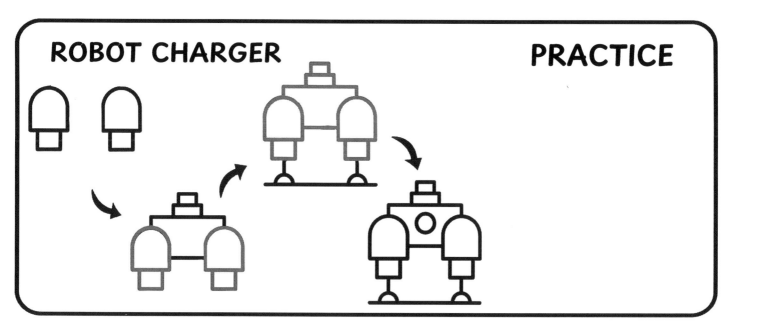
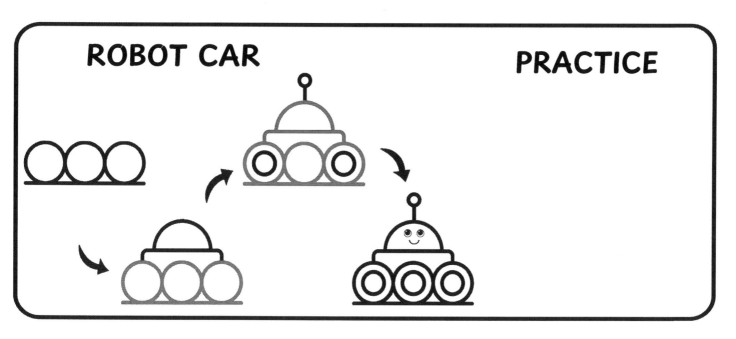
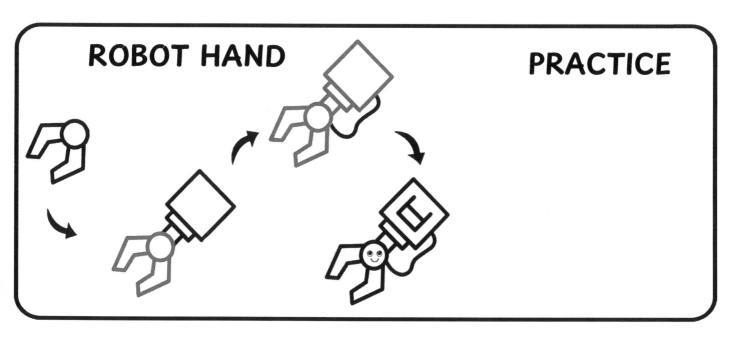

SUNNY RAINBOW — PRACTICE

CHICKEN — PRACTICE

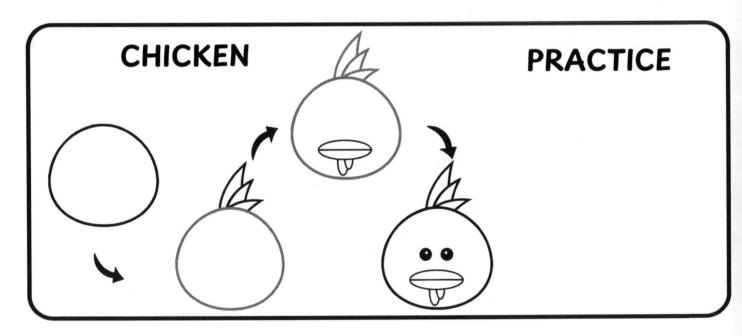

ROBOT — PRACTICE

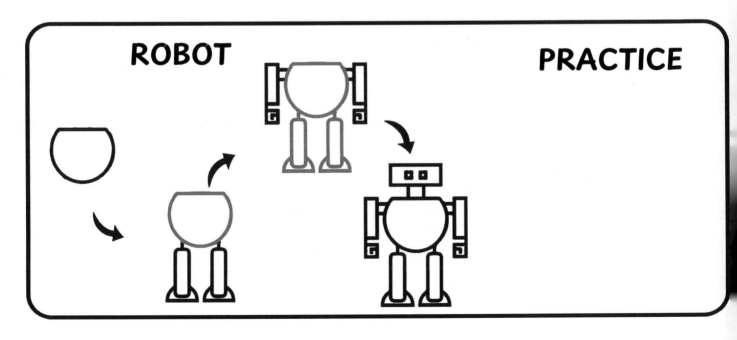

FLOWER SHAPE — PRACTICE

TRIANGLE SHAPE — PRACTICE

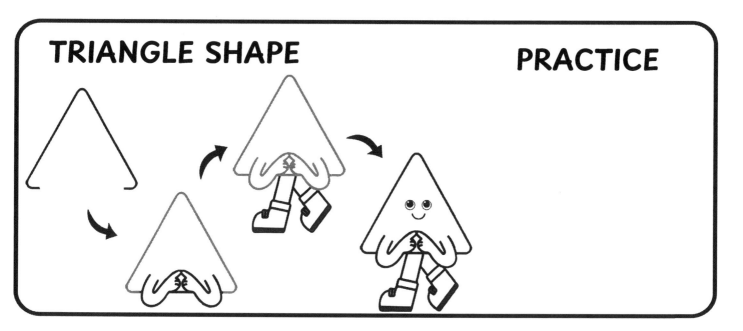

CIRCLE SHAPE — PRACTICE

Chapter 5: Toys and Accessories

SURF BOARD — PRACTICE

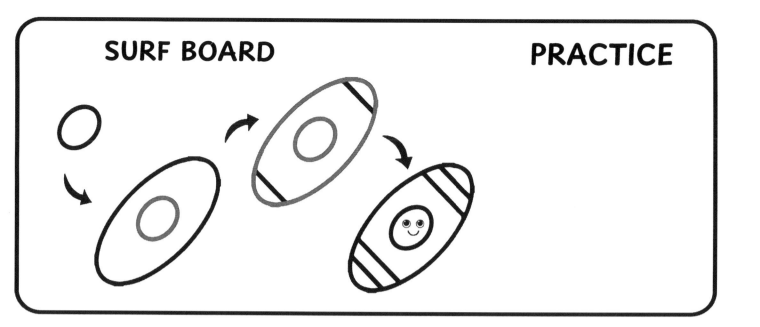

OVEN — PRACTICE

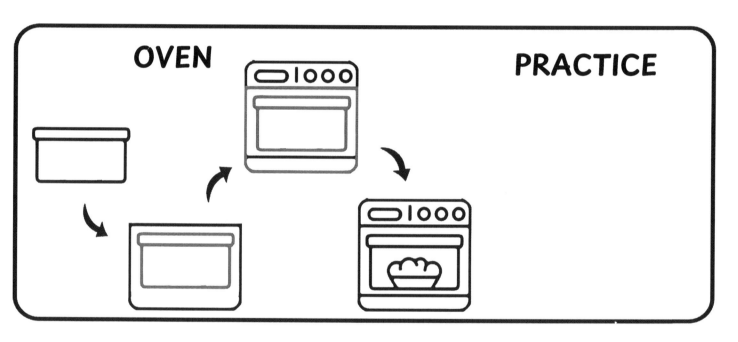

WORK AT HOME — PRACTICE

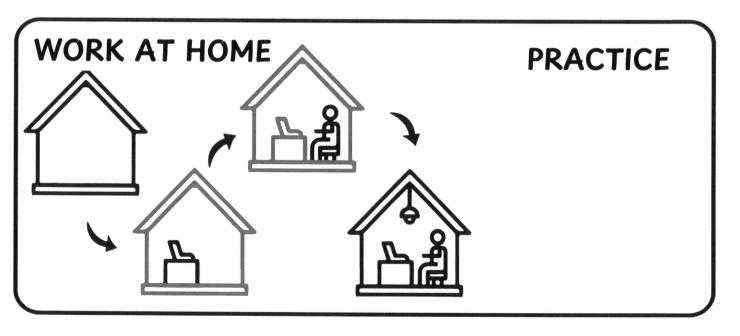

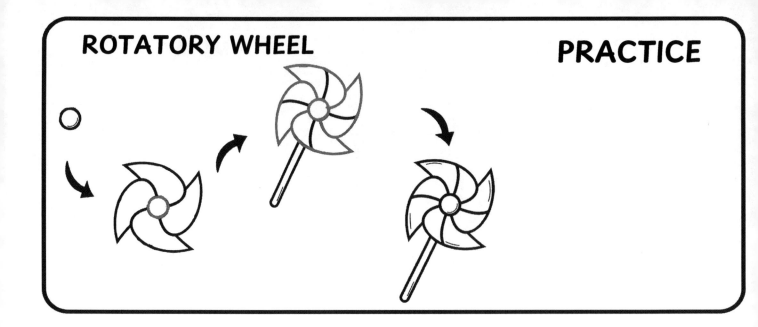

ROTATORY WHEEL — PRACTICE

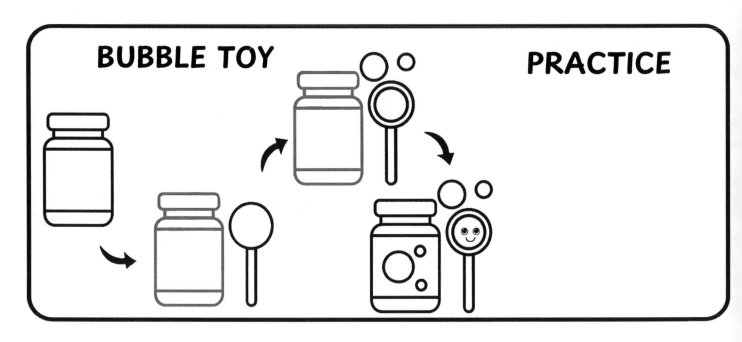

BUBBLE TOY — PRACTICE

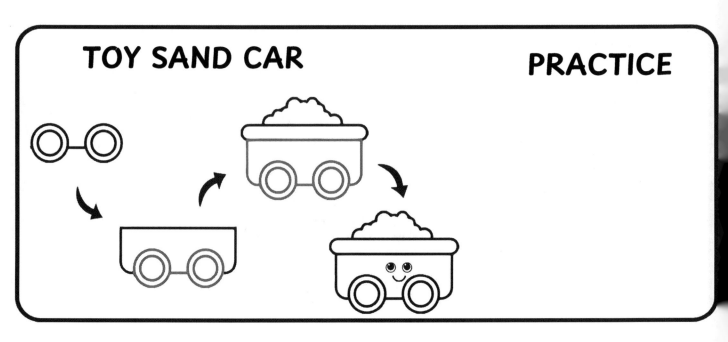

TOY SAND CAR — PRACTICE

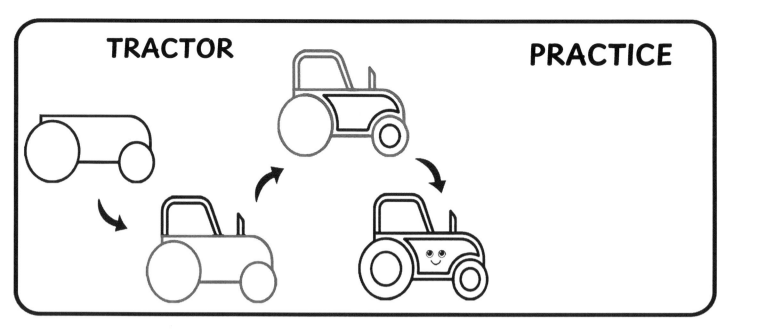

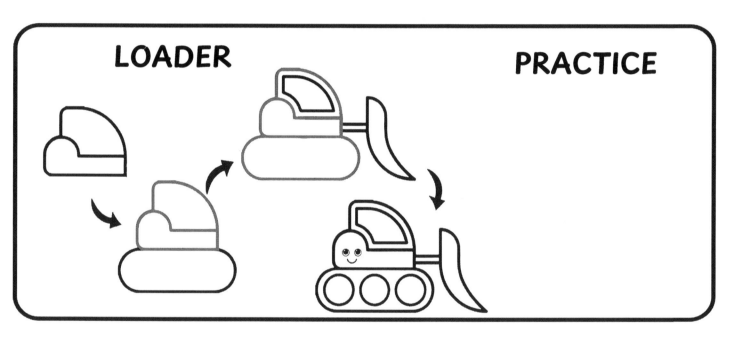

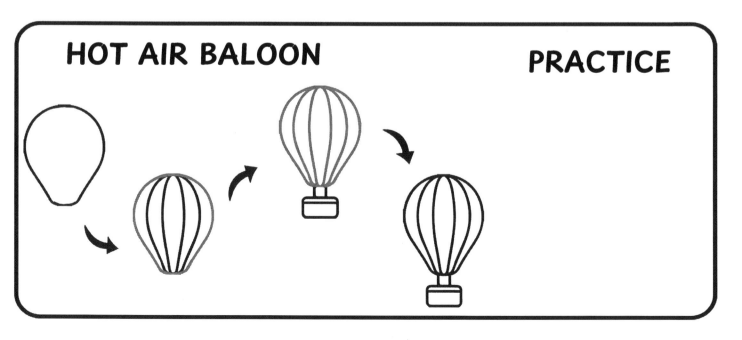

CAR TOY PRACTICE

LANTERN PRACTICE

ROCKET TOY PRACTICE

ROCKT — PRACTICE

TEDDY BEAR — PRACTICE

DOG IN LUGGAGE RACK — PRACTICE

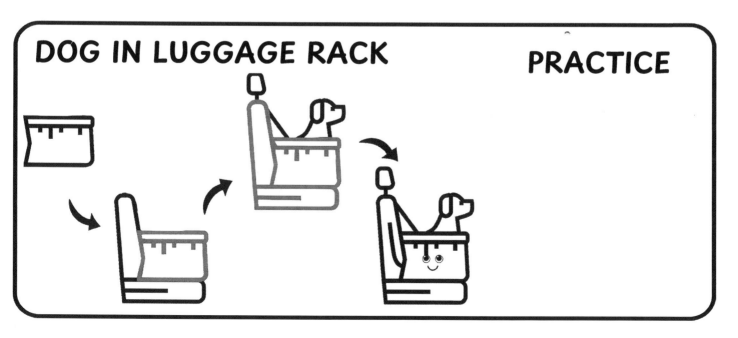

BROOM PRACTICE

CHIMNEY PRACTICE

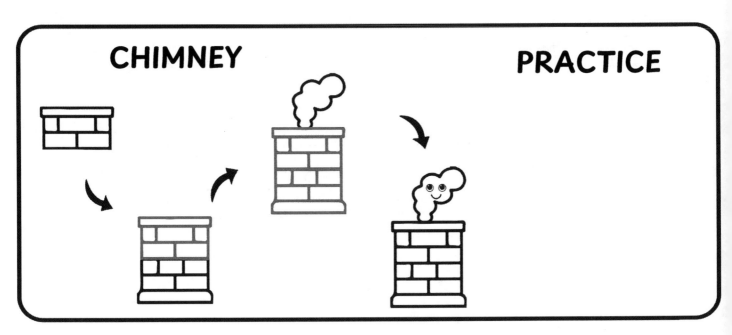

HUT PRACTICE

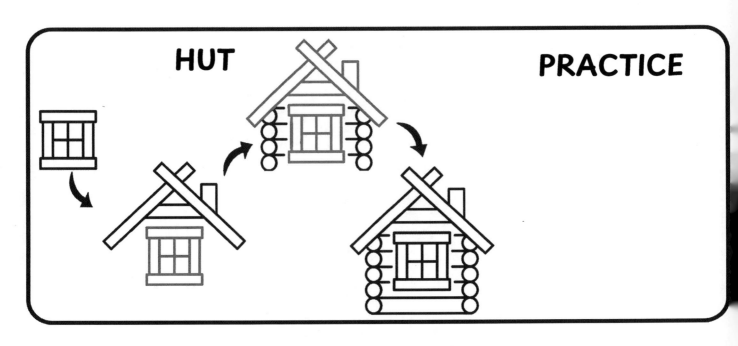

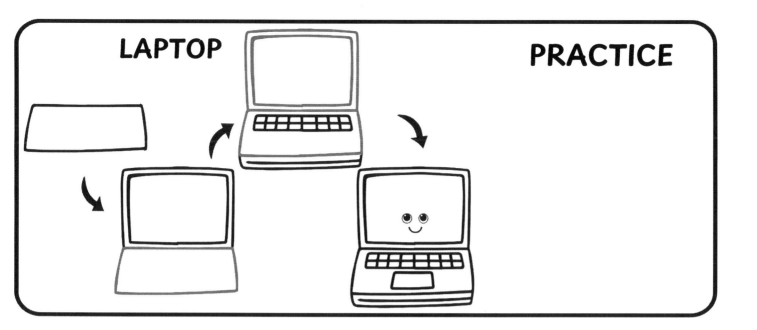

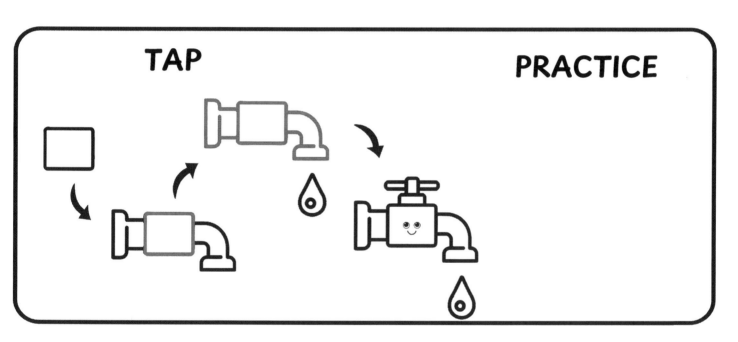

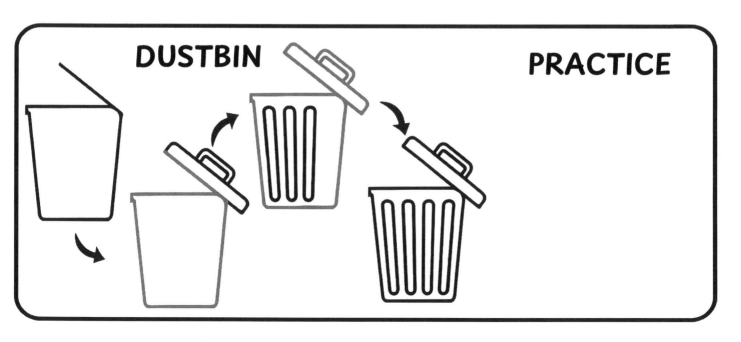

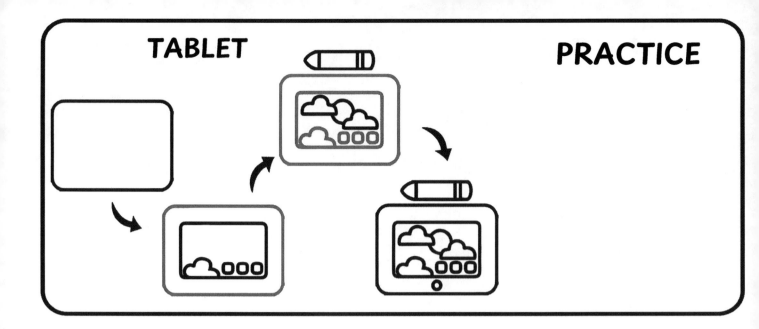
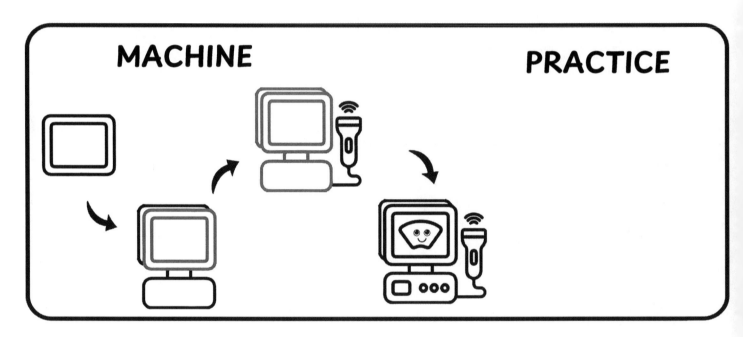
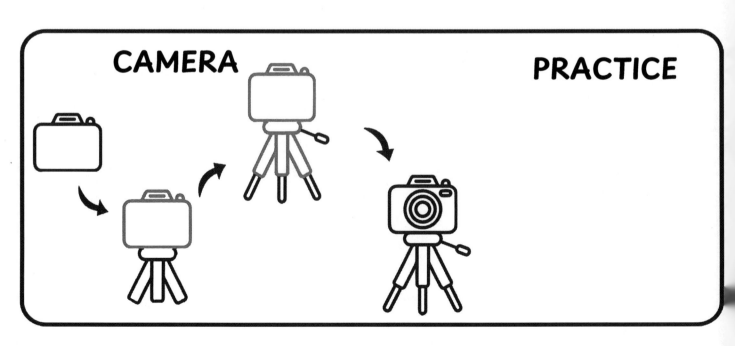

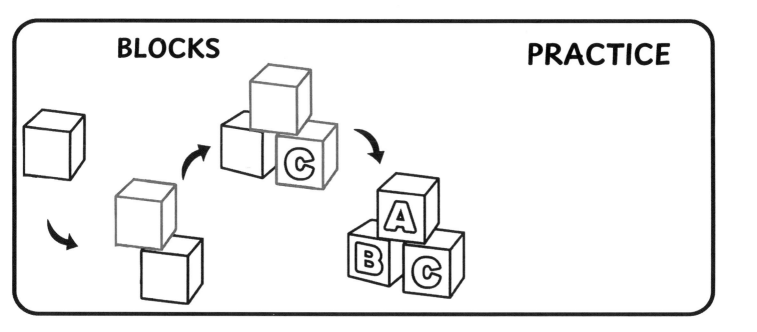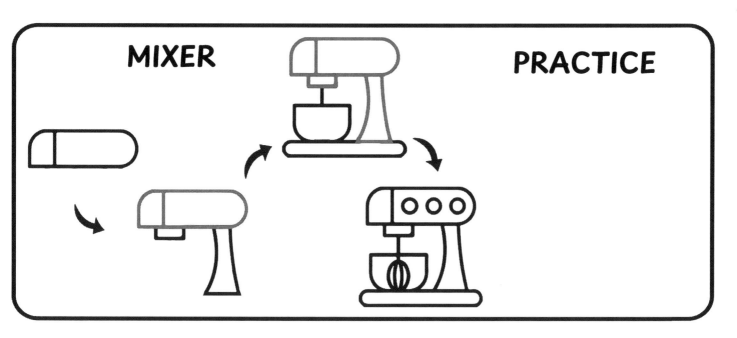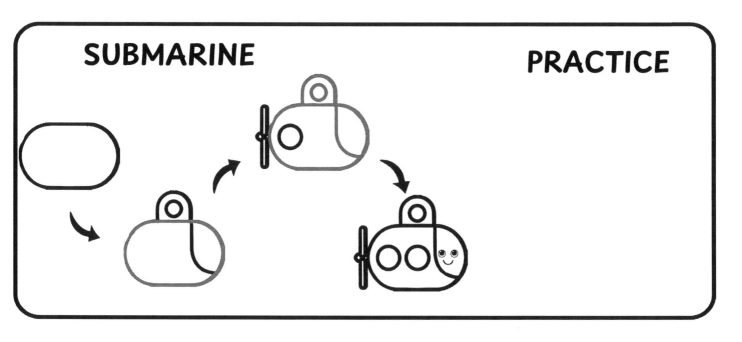

LAMP PRACTICE

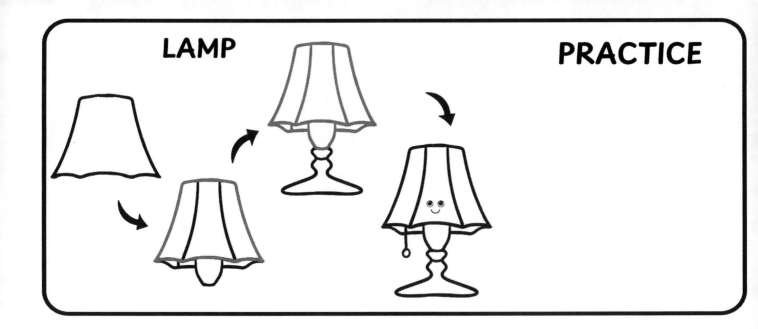

BED PRACTICE

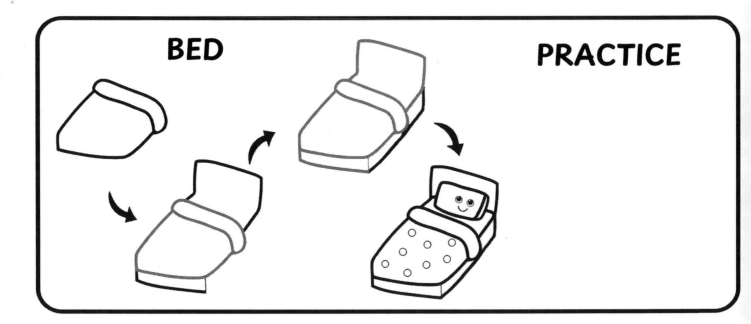

SOFA PRACTICE

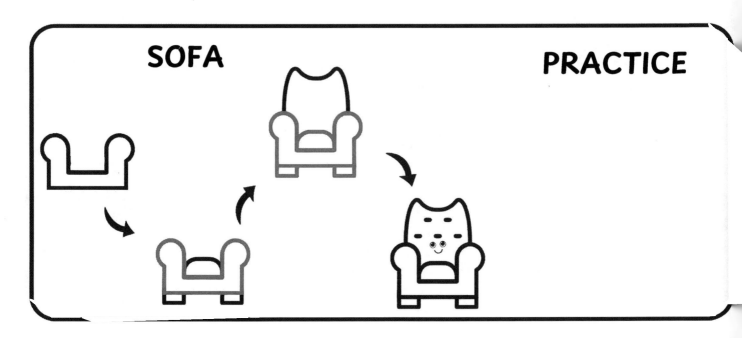

PICKUP PRACTICE

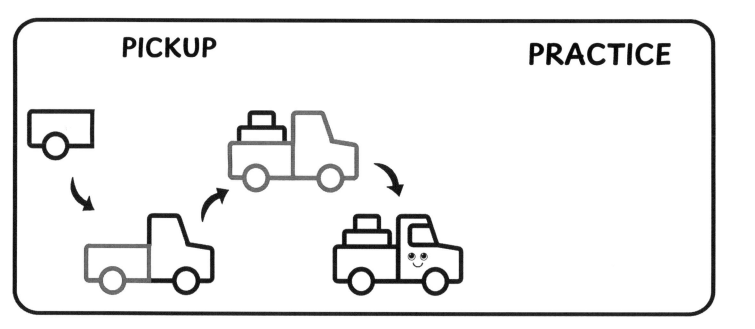

TRAIN PRACTICE

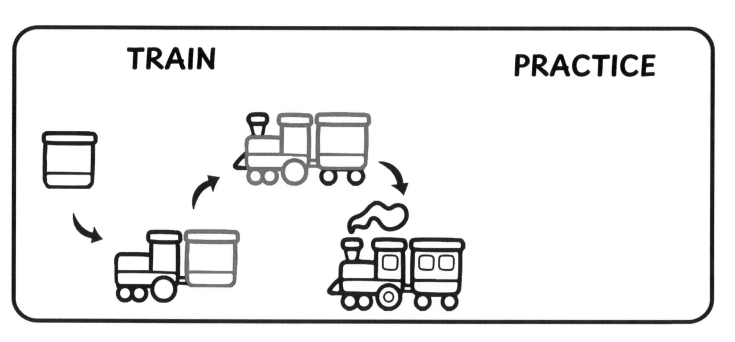

CAR PRACTICE

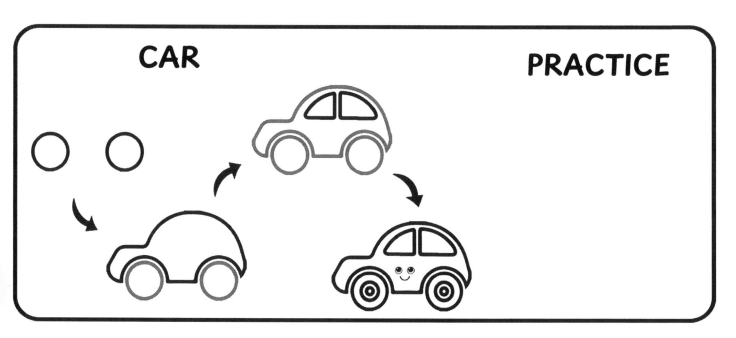

SHIRT — PRACTICE

BUBBLE GUN TOY — PRACTICE

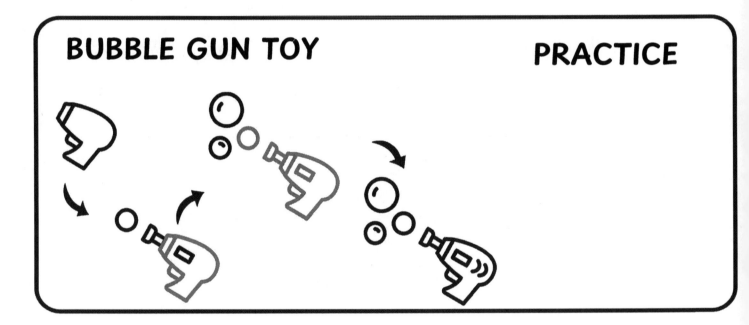

MARKERS — PRACTICE

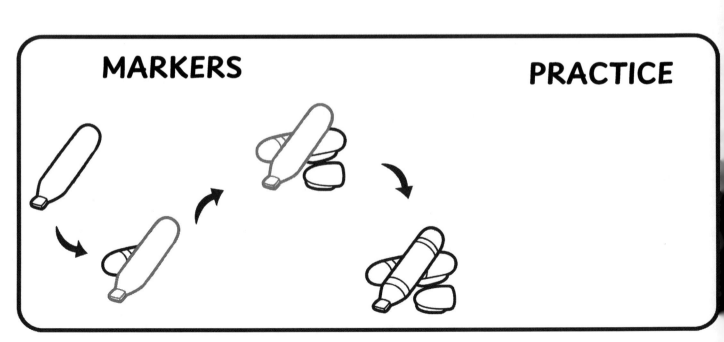

CRAYON PRACTICE

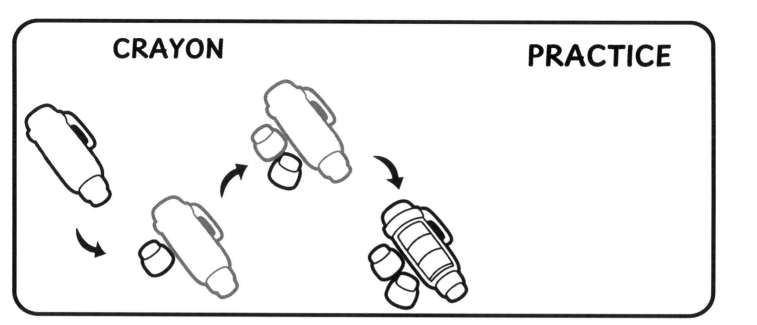

BOWLING PRACTICE

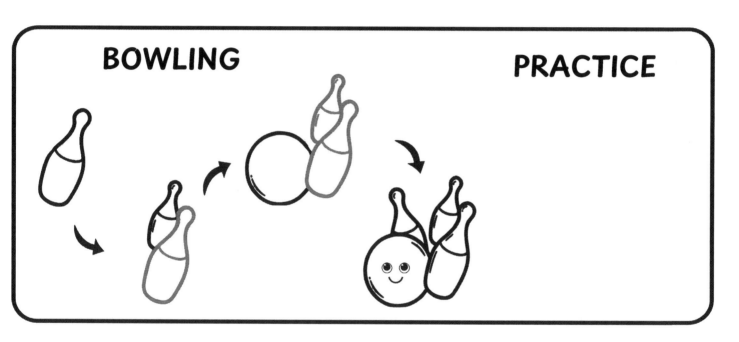

BAG PRACTICE

XYLOPHONE PRACTICE

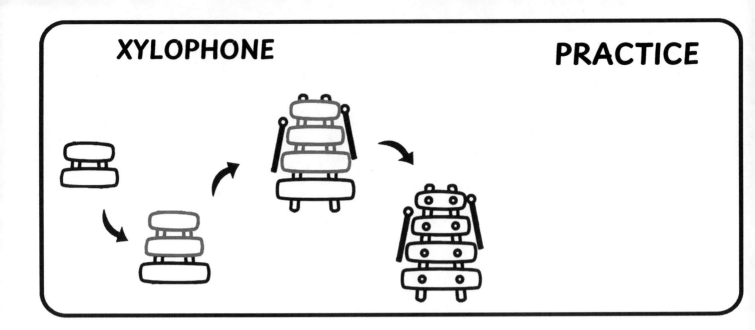

OVEN PRACTICE

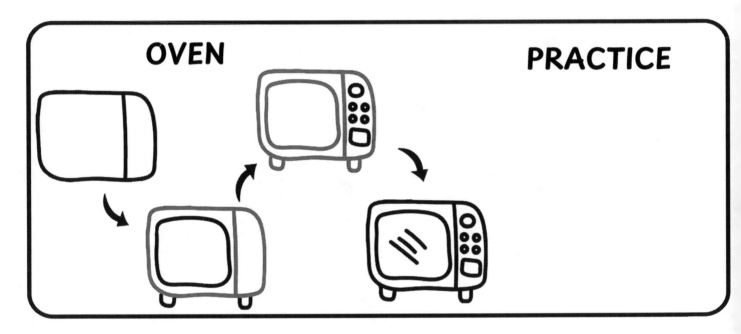

ROCKING HORSE PRACTICE

FLOWER POT — PRACTICE

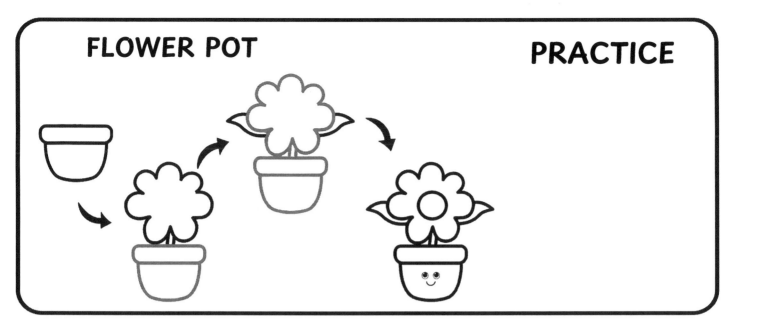

LILY — PRACTICE

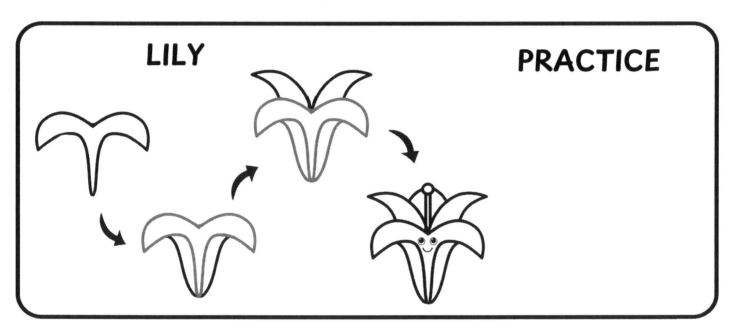

FLOWER — PRACTICE

Leave a Review & Showcase your Artwork!

Our Creative Readers

Thank you for joining us on this colorful journey! We hope this book has sparked your imagination and brought joy to your creative time. Remember, your art is as unique as you are, and every masterpiece tells a story.

We'd love to see your incredible creations! Share your favorite works and leave a review to inspire others. Your feedback helps us continue creating books that ignite creativity and bring happiness to children everywhere.

Keep exploring, keep creating, and always let your imagination soar!

With love and creativity,
Lyra Venn

Made in the USA
Columbia, SC
16 June 2025